# WINNING ON THE

# INSIDE

BY

# CHARLES F. STANLEY

THOMAS NELSON
*Since 1798*

Winning on the Inside

Charles F. Stanley

Copyright © 1998, 2008 by Charles F. Stanley

Published in Nashville, Tennessee, by Thomas Nelson, Inc.

Editing, layout, and design by Gregory C. Benoit Publishing, Old Mystic, CT

ISBN-13: 978-1-4185-2816-4

Printed in the United States of America

09 10 11 12 QW 6 5 4 3

# Contents

INTRODUCTION
**Taking a Fresh Look at Temptation** .......................................1

LESSON 1
**Facing Temptation**...........................................................3

LESSON 2
**The Big Picture**............................................................10

LESSON 3
**Who's to Blame?** ..........................................................22

LESSON 4
**The Appeal**...............................................................34

LESSON 5
**Our Defender**.............................................................50

LESSON 6
**Avoiding the Danger Zones**...............................................62

LESSON 7
**Dressed for Battle**........................................................73

LESSON 8
**Wielding the Sword** .......................................................85

LESSON 9
**No Lone Rangers** .........................................................99

LESSON 10
**Misunderstandings About Temptation**............................ 108

# Taking a Fresh Look at Temptation

Most people believe that they have a fairly good grasp of what it means to be tempted. They have faced temptation in their lives, and they know the right response to temptation: say no! Most people want to say no to temptation. But most people also admit that they frequently give in to temptation, and they bear guilt about doing so. What these people do not know, in part, is the *whole* of what the Bible has to say about temptation and how to overcome it.

The Bible is not merely a book of "do's" and "don'ts," but a book of "how to's." It is an extremely practical book with truth that can be applied directly to daily situations and circumstances. The Bible tells us to "yield not" to temptation, but it also tells us *how* to avoid yielding and how to avoid temptation in the first place.

The Bible is also a book of spiritual inspiration. It motivates us, compels us, and encourages us. It gives us the "want to" outlook that we need if we are to overcome temptation. There simply is no better resource on how to overcome temptation than the Holy Bible. As you begin this study, I encourage you to set aside what you believe the Bible says on the subject of temptation and inner struggles. As much as possible, approach the Scriptures with fresh spiritual eyes and ears. Let the Bible speak to you in a new way.

This book can be used by you alone or by several people in a small-group study. At various times, you will be asked to relate to the material in one of these four ways:

1. *What new insights have you gained?* Make notes about the insights that you have. You may want to record them in your Bible or in a separate journal. As you reflect back over your insights, you are likely to see how God has moved in your life.

2. *Have you ever had a similar experience?* Each of us approaches the Bible from a unique background—our own particular set of relationships and experiences. Our experiences do not make the Bible true— the Word of God is truth regardless of our opinion about it. It is important, however, to share our experiences in order to see how God's truth can be applied to human lives.

3. *How do you feel about the material presented?* Emotional responses do not give validity to the Scriptures, nor should we trust our emotions as a gauge for our faith. In small-group Bible study, however, it is good for participants to express their emotions. The Holy Spirit often communicates with us through this unspoken language.

4. *In what way do you feel challenged to respond or to act?* God's Word may cause you to feel inspired or challenged to change something in your life. Take the challenge seriously and find ways of acting upon it. If God reveals to you a particular need that He wants *you* to address, take that as "marching orders" from God. God is expecting you to *do* something with the challenge that He has just given you.

Start and conclude your Bible study sessions in prayer. Ask God to give you spiritual eyes to see and spiritual ears to hear. As you conclude your study, ask the Lord to seal what you have learned so that you will never forget it. Ask Him to help you grow into the fullness of the stature of Christ Jesus.

I caution you to keep the Bible at the center of your study. A genuine Bible study stays focused on God's Word and promotes a growing faith and a closer walk with the Holy Spirit in *each* person who participates.

# LESSON 1

# Facing Temptation

┌─────────────── ☙ **In This Lesson** ❧ ───────────────┐

LEARNING: IS TEMPTATION REALLY SUCH A BIG DEAL?

GROWING: IF IT MATTERS, THEN HOW DO I OVERCOME TEMPTATION?

───────────── ∞ ─────────────
└──────────────────────────────────────────────────────┘

When you hear the word *temptation,* what flashes into your mind? What pictures and emotions does this word conjure up in your thinking? For some, temptation means a delicious hot fudge sundae with whipped cream and nuts dripping off the sides. For others, it's the man or woman who has become the focus of secret fantasies at the office. For the teenager, the word may bring to mind a can of beer or a pack of cigarettes or a member of the opposite sex who has been declared off-limits by parents.

To what does *your* imagination turn when you think of temptation? This is a very important question as we begin a study on this topic. In a sense, whatever comes to your mind is what this book is about. Our concern is not with *what* tempts us, but with *who* tempts us and how we are to respond to temptation.

For many people, the prospects of overcoming temptation seem slim. They say, "I've tried and failed so many times before. Why frustrate myself all over again?" There are several reasons why we must never give up in our struggle against temptation.

# Fight the Fight

*First, if you don't struggle against temptation, a defeating habit will take root and rob you of your confidence in the power of God in your life.* You will feel disheartened and may even come to believe that God does not love you or that He has abandoned you in your struggles in life. At that point, you are in danger of developing what the Bible calls a "hard heart."

A hard heart develops when people hear and believe the truth, but refuse to apply it. It is a process that occurs over time, but it follows a fairly predictable pattern: a Christian recognizes sin in his life, feels convicted about it, does nothing about it, and becomes less sensitive to the prompting of the Holy Spirit. At that point, he becomes callous and begins to "quench" the work of the Holy Spirit in his life (see 1 Thessalonians 5:19). That is a very dangerous position to be in.

The person who develops a hard heart loses all moral and ethical direction, insofar as the Holy Spirit is concerned. To be adrift without a moral compass is a highly unsatisfying way to live. It truly is a life without meaningful reward.

A failure to fight against temptation can lead to a great gulf of separation from God. The pattern is evident in countless lives. When we refuse to confront temptation and struggle against it, we begin to cut ourselves off from the spiritual lifeline of God's power in our lives. God loves us still. God remains available to us. But *we* have turned away from God so that He no longer can work in us and through us to the extent He desires.

## ∞ Share the Good News ∞

*Second, if you refuse to engage in a battle against temptation and you lose confidence in God's power and presence in your life, you will be hesitant to offer Christ as the answer to others who are controlled by sin.* Your witness for Christ will be deeply affected. One of the immediate results of being set free from a controlling habit is the desire to share the power of God that has set you free. Satan loves to keep us in bondage to sin because our potential for the kingdom of God is greatly diminished.

## ∞ Temptation Spreads ∞

*Third, if you fail to engage in a battle against temptation to commit one type of sin, you likely will find yourself more prone to engage in other types of sin.* We've all heard the phrase, "One sin leads to another." Sin is like a cancer that spreads. One area that is not dealt with opens up other areas as well. Once you become accustomed to a particular sin and it becomes entrenched in your lifestyle, it is only a matter of time until other areas become problems.

## ∞ Sin Leads to Death ∞

*Fourth, if you fail to engage in a battle against temptation, you ultimately will experience death of some type.* James 1:14–16 tells us,

> But each one is tempted when he is drawn away by his own desires and enticed. Then, when desire has conceived, it gives birth to sin; and sin, when it is full-grown, brings forth death. Do not be deceived, my beloved brethren.

James gives us an equation: Temptation + Sin = Death. Whenever sin manifests itself, some type of death results. Destructive habits take root. The result may be a physical death, usually over time. The sin may bring about a death to a relationship, a death to part of your emotional or psychological capacity, a death of reputation, a death of integrity, a death of a career, a death of loyalty or respect. Something is always destroyed when sin is allowed to go unchecked.

## Take Temptation Seriously

If temptation has such deadly consequences, why is it that so many people do not take temptation more seriously? One of the foremost reasons is that we have excused our failures by saying, "I'm only human. Nobody's perfect."

There is truth in both statements, of course. The greater truth of God's Word, however, is that we are human and imperfect yet we are given free will. We have the potential to say no to temptation. We have the ability to confront and overcome temptation as imperfect human beings. The real issue is whether we choose to have the *desire* to overcome temptation.

### ∞ The Core of Pride ∞

At the core of our reluctance to confront temptation seems to be a greater issue: pride. We want what we want. We do not want to be conformed to the image of Christ Jesus. We do not want to live in accordance with God's commandments when our own pleasure seems to be at stake. A struggle against temptation requires that we do two things:

1. Choose God's way over our own way.

2. Trust in God to help us succeed in choosing His way.

We'll discuss both of those requirements later in this study, but it is important to recognize at the outset that the struggle against temptation is not a light issue. It goes to the very core of our spiritual identity.

All of this may sound overly serious to you. You may be saying, "But my particular problem is not nearly as big as the ones that you seem to allude to." If that is the case, great! The best time to deal with temptation is before it takes root in your life and grows into a habit that controls you. As a pastor, I have heard countless stories about how "little" habits turned into bigger ones that resulted in great and widespread devastation. I've heard how marriages, businesses, families, and lives were destroyed, and in tracing back through the questions of what happened and what caused it, a very simple action could nearly always be pinpointed that was contrary to God's plan. It may have been only an offhand, careless remark of one spouse to another, a few minutes of looking at pornographic material, the first theft of a few dollars from the company's petty cash, the first drink at a neighborhood bar, the first conversation with a person met at a truck stop. Little temptations *can* become big sins.

As we begin a closer look at the subject of temptation, I want to applaud you for undertaking this study. It takes courage to admit to temptation, to face it, and to defeat it. I have great faith that God will bless you as you engage in this study, and that you will find a new inner strength to overcome temptation and to truly live a victorious life. Winning on the inside is the most important "winning" that you can do!

☙ In what areas have you struggled with temptation in the past? Is there one specific temptation that you confront repeatedly?

☙ Are you challenged to grow in your relationship with the Lord? Do you feel challenged to confront temptation with new resolve?

But each one is tempted when he is drawn away by his own desires and enticed. Then, when desire has conceived, it gives birth to sin; and sin, when it is full-grown, brings forth death.

—James 1:14-15

☙ Give real-life examples of James' sequence: desire conceives temptation; temptation gives birth to sin; sin grows into death.

~ When have your own desires led you into temptation? At what point does a desire become a temptation? At what point does a temptation become a sin?

---

## ~ Today and Tomorrow ~

TODAY: RESISTING TEMPTATION IS EXTREMELY IMPORTANT IN THE CHRISTIAN LIFE.

TOMORROW: I WILL SPEND TIME THIS WEEK PRAYING AND SEARCHING MY OWN LIFE TO CONFRONT THE THINGS THAT TEMPT ME.

---

## ~ Notes and Prayer Requests: ~

LESSON 2

# The Big Picture

---------------- ❧ **In This Lesson** ❧ ----------------

LEARNING: WHERE DOES TEMPTATION COME FROM IN THE FIRST PLACE?

GROWING: WHAT DIFFERENCE DOES IT MAKE TO ANYONE ELSE WHETHER
OR NOT I RESIST?

---------------- ❧ ----------------

Most of us learn best with a sort of "telescope" and "microscope" approach. At times we need to look very closely at something, almost to the point of dissecting it. At other times, we benefit by getting the "big picture" and seeing how details relate to a larger whole.

It is important for us to realize that our individual temptations have a much broader context. You may think that your struggle with temptation does not matter to anybody but you, but it does. Your struggle is not an isolated struggle. Our heavenly Father takes very seriously every victory or defeat in the life of an individual believer, in part because that struggle is part of a much greater struggle.

## Order Out of Disorder

The creation account in Genesis describes how God brought order out of disorder, something out of nothing.

In the beginning God created the heavens and the earth. The earth was *without form, and void; and darkness was on the face of the deep.* And the Spirit of God was hovering over the face of the waters. Then God said, "Let there be light"; and there was light.

—Genesis 1:1–3 *(emphasis added)*

The earth was formless, and God gave it form. The world was in darkness, and God brought forth light. The creation of man was the apex of that creation—man was given a very special role to fill:

Then God said, "Let Us make man in Our image, according to Our likeness; let them have dominion over the fish of the sea, over the birds of the air, and over the cattle, over all the earth and over every creeping thing that creeps on the earth."

–Genesis 1:26

Man was then blessed and told to multiply, fill the earth, and subdue it (see Genesis 1:28). He was given authority over all life—both the plants and the animals. To ensure that man was equipped for the job of ruling His creation, God created him *in God's image* and *according to God's likeness.* Man, unlike any other part of creation, shared with God an intellect, a will, emotions, an ability to reason and make decisions, and an ability to love, obey, and disobey. All of these are vital to ruling creation the way that God ordained.

11

Then God saw everything that He had made, and indeed it was very good. So the evening and the morning were the sixth day.

—Genesis 1:31

☙ Notice in Genesis 1 that God describes everything as "good" until He had completed creation on the sixth day. Why does He then declare all creation to be "very good"?

☙ God created everything to be perfect—it was Adam's sin that brought sin and death into the world. What does this suggest about your own natural desires?

## Adam's Sin

But Adam plunged mankind and all of creation into a tailspin by his willful disobedience of God. The world was thrown into a state of up-heaval, both morally and physically. This disobedience was rooted in Satan's *tempting* Eve and, through her, Adam. Why was Satan so intent upon tempting Adam to sin? What was at stake for him?

The prophets Isaiah and Ezekiel give us brief descriptions of a cosmic war that took place some time before the creation of the world. According to their accounts, Satan at one time held a very high position in the kingdom of heaven. Here is what Ezekiel tells us (Ezekiel 28:14–15):

You were the anointed cherub who covers;
I established you;
You were on the holy mountain of God;
You walked back and forth in the midst of fiery stones.
You were perfect in your ways from the day you were created,
Till iniquity was found in you.

Satan became filled with pride and decided that he should be God. Isaiah tells us (14:13–14):

For you have said in your heart:
"I will ascend into heaven,
I will exalt my throne above the stars of God;
I will also sit on the mount of the congregation
On the farthest sides of the north;
I will ascend above the heights of the clouds,
I will be like the Most High."

What followed was a battle that resulted in Satan's being cast out of heaven along with those angels that chose to side with him. Ezekiel tells us that he was cast to the ground—the earth (see 28:17). Why would God allow Satan to live on this earth? His presence here is part of God's provision for man's free will. If man did not have the opportunity to disobey or to follow Satan, he would not truly have free will. Each of us has been given the opportunity to choose whom we will follow and obey.

Satan knows that to defeat man is to defeat all of God's creation on this earth. Satan's attack on mankind was simply his way of striking back at God, intending to reverse God's will and plunge all of earth into chaos. Satan seeks revenge against God and a return to the power that he once knew—and even more so, he seeks to gain power that he never had.

All of creation has suffered since the day that Adam sinned. Paul wrote in Romans 8:19–22:

> For the earnest expectation of the creation eagerly waits for the revealing of the sons of God. For the creation was subjected to futility, not willingly, but because of Him who subjected it in hope; because the creation itself also will be delivered from the bondage of corruption into the glorious liberty of the children of God. For we know that the whole creation groans and labors with birth pangs together until now.

What does Paul mean when he says that "the creation was subjected to futility"? What does this suggest about your natural desires?

Notice that Paul uses the same birth imagery that James uses (see Lesson 1). If temptation gives birth to sin (James 1:14-15), what "birth pangs" is Paul referring to here?

14

# Sin Causes Decay and Death

Sin is an agent of decay. Once sin is introduced into anything—an individual, a relationship, a community—order and productivity begin to diminish. Goodness declines.

Evil is not a thing; it is a *lack* of perfection. God's creation was perfect, and evil is a process of ruining that perfection and detracting from it. We can look back over history at what resulted when sin was introduced into the world. First, God's order of authority was broken. Man had set himself up to be his own god. We have countless illustrations that show a perpetual slide from order to disorder, from creation as God intended it to chaos. The battle initiated by Satan continues to rage.

If God had not stepped into history, all of creation might very well have destroyed itself. In Genesis 6:5–8 we read:

> Then the LORD saw that the wickedness of man was great in the earth, and that every intent of the thoughts of his heart was only evil continually. And the LORD was sorry that He had made man on the earth, and He was grieved in His heart. So the LORD said, "I will destroy man whom I have created from the face of the earth, both man and beast, creeping thing and birds of the air, for I am sorry that I have made them." But Noah found grace in the eyes of the LORD.

God began again, but the problem of a sin nature remained in mankind. To deal with that problem, God sent Jesus to die for man's sin. Through Christ Jesus, men and women have the opportunity to deal with both the penalty and the power of sin in their lives. When we come to Christ, God gains a definitive victory over Satan in our lives. Satan has "lost" us and God has "found" us. We are squarely planted on the winning side of eternity.

Up to the point that we accepted Christ as our personal Savior, we experienced many temptations, and we had no certain and lasting means of overcoming those temptations. We were "bent" toward sin; we had a natural inclination to sin. Satan was manipulating us to his side. But once we accepted Christ as our personal Savior and received the Holy Spirit into our lives, we were given a "bent" toward what is right before God. We were given a desire to live our lives in a way that is pleasing and good in God's eyes.

When a person is truly born again, he will have no desire to sin. He will *want* to do what is right. Furthermore, he will grow in the grace and knowledge of the Lord Jesus Christ. He will be on a path of life—an abundant life now and an eternal life after our physical death.

> What shall we say then? Shall we continue in sin that grace may abound? Certainly not! How shall we who died to sin live any longer in it? Or do you not know that as many of us as were baptized into Christ Jesus were baptized into His death? Therefore we were buried with Him through baptism into death, that just as Christ was raised from the dead by the glory of the Father, even so we also should walk in newness of life.
>
> —Romans 6:1-4

Imagine that you suddenly dropped dead. What effect would temptation have upon you then? How do these verses relate to that image?

❧ What does it mean to "walk in newness of life"? In what ways is this the positive aspect of being "dead to sin"?

# A New Process Toward Life

We must be very clear on this point: before an individual places his trust in Christ, he is constantly decaying. He is headed for eternal death. However, once an individual has placed his trust in Christ and has been born anew spiritually, a new process goes into effect. That individual is indwelled by the Holy Spirit, and the chaotic cycle of sin is reversed into a cycle that promotes life. As the apostle Paul wrote in 2 Corinthians 4:16:

> Therefore we do not lose heart. Even though our outward man is perishing, yet the inward man is being renewed day by day.

We are new creatures on the inside. This renewal process enables us to overcome even strong temptations to sin—if we will put our trust in Christ to help us overcome temptation.

Decay happens over time, and a total renewal of the inner person also happens over time. This does not mean that our salvation is uncertain. When a person accepts Jesus as Savior, he is born anew, and what is "birthed" cannot be unbirthed. The Holy Spirit does not depart from that person. Eternal life is guaranteed to him—automatically, definitively, and without compromise (see John 3:16).

A holy and righteous life, however, is not automatic. A struggle continues because we still live in physical, earthly bodies that have not been fully redeemed from sin's influence. We must actively put on the new identity in thought, word, and deed that God has ordained for us. We must experience a total renewal of our minds and hearts.

> ...put off, concerning your former conduct, the old man which grows corrupt according to the deceitful lusts, and be renewed in the spirit of your mind, and that you put on the new man which was created according to God, in true righteousness and holiness.
>
> —Ephesians 4:22-24

❧ Give practical examples of what your "old man" was like in "your former conduct".

❧ Give examples of ways that you can "put on the new man".

# Why Do Satan's Temptations Continue?

Satan tempts us, even though we belong to God, for two reasons. First, if he can't have you, he'll do his best to discourage you and to make you miserable as long as you live on earth. Satan seeks to inflict as much pain and misery as possible. He never ceases to be an oppressor.

Second, Satan will do his best to keep you from being an effective witness to others. If he can succeed in making you an ineffective witness—destroying your reputation, causing you to live under a cloud of guilt and depression, causing you to sin blatantly before others—he has hope that you will *not* influence others to accept Jesus Christ as their Savior. He knows that, if he can get you caught up in sin—however small it may be—you are sidelined as far as the kingdom of God is concerned. Every victory that Satan has over you is a minor victory in thwarting the advancement of God's kingdom.

Our struggle with temptation, therefore, is not limited to ourselves. It is a struggle that is part of a much greater struggle between God and Satan and between those who believe in Jesus Christ and the one who would seek to destroy them. Paul is very clear about this in Ephesians 6:12:

> For we do not wrestle against flesh and blood, but against principalities, against powers, against the rulers of the darkness of this age, against spiritual hosts of wickedness in the heavenly places.

Each one of our struggles has a spiritual core to it. Each battle against temptation—each choice that we make for good or for evil—is part of an ongoing struggle between the kingdom of God and the kingdom of Satan. That's the big picture which we must keep in mind if we are to become victorious over temptation. We are not winning for ourselves alone; our victory is part of a much bigger and eternal victory.

⮞ When have you realized that your temptations were a "wrestling" against "the rulers of darkness"?

⮞ If we are wrestling against the powers of darkness in this world, what does that suggest about the importance of resisting temptation?

Therefore, if anyone is in Christ, he is a new creation; old things have passed away; behold, all things have become new.

—2 Corinthians 5:17

⮞ How does this verse relate to the "new nature" which you received when you became a Christian?

If you have a new, Christ-like nature, what does that mean about the things that used to tempt you?

## Today and Tomorrow

*TODAY:* SINS—EVEN LITTLE ONES—HAVE AN EFFECT ON THE PEOPLE AROUND ME, AND GIVE A VICTORY TO SATAN.

*TOMORROW:* I WILL ASK THE LORD TO SHOW ME WAYS THAT I CAN BRING HIM THE GLORY THIS WEEK: BY RESISTING TEMPTATION.

## Notes and Prayer Requests:

# LESSON 3

# Who's to Blame?

─────────── ❧ In This Lesson ❧ ───────────

LEARNING: WHAT ABOUT TEMPTATIONS THAT GROW OUT OF MY CHILD-
HOOD?

GROWING: IS IT REALLY SIN IF IT'S LEGAL AND ACCEPTED IN MY CULTURE?

─────────── ⸎ ───────────

Most of us have no genuine desire to take responsibility for our own temptation. We'd much rather find someone else to blame. We hear countless stories today of people who attempt to justify their sins by blaming their childhood, their parents, their genetic code, the government, specific situations, their employers, and even God.

This tendency to "pass the buck" is certainly nothing new. It started with the line used by Adam: "The woman whom You gave to be with me, she gave me of the tree, and I ate" (Genesis 3:12). It was perpetuated by Eve, who said to God: "The serpent deceived me, and I ate" (Genesis 3:13).

Adam tried placing the blame on another person. Eve tried placing the blame on the devil. Neither justification kept Adam and Eve from being accountable for their own actions.

☜ What excuses have you attempted to give for your sin?

☜ When has someone else tried to blame you for his own sinful actions?

Blaming someone else for your weakness appears to take the responsibility from your shoulders. But by mentally removing yourself from responsibility, you are also removing yourself from correcting the situation. Until you are willing to take responsibility for your own sins, you will be unwilling—and therefore unable—to do anything about them. In this lesson, I want to take a look at several of the foremost excuses that people use to justify their weakness in the face of temptation.

### ∞ "That's Just the Way I Am" ∞

Many people blame their personalities for their inability to deal with temptations. They say, "I've always been this way" or "That's just the way I am." The implication in these statements is also, "This is the way I will always be." In making such a statement, we are actually asking God to take the blame for our sins. We are saying, in effect, "If You hadn't made me this way, God, I wouldn't do this."

The fact is, you *learned* how to sin. You had a built-in tendency to sin, but at some point you learned and then *chose* to sin. In most cases, sin has become a bad habit. You do what you do because you have always done what you do. That does not mean, however, that you *must* do what you do or that you cannot change what you do.

God made you with many talents and desires. He expected you to use your innate gifts for His purposes and His glory. He expected you to use all that you are and have for *good*, not evil. Your choice of behavior is just that—*your choice.*

✎ What behavior in your life would you most like to blame on somebody else? Is that an indication to you of a particular area of weakness in your life?

Ponder the path of your feet, And let all your ways be established. Do not turn to the right or the left; Remove your foot from evil.

—Proverbs 4:26-27

&. Why does Solomon speak of our "feet" rather than of our hands or hearts? What does this suggest about the temptations that we "find ourselves in"?

&. Why does he say, "remove your foot from evil"? What does *this* suggest about temptations that we "find ourselves in"?

### ∞ "Everybody is Doing It" ∞

Many people think that there's safety in numbers—if everybody is engaging in their particular brand of sin, then it must be all right. Nothing could be farther from the truth. God does not grade on the curve or give in to the popular wishes of men and women. His commandments and His promises are absolute.

If God says yes to something, He means yes. If He says no, He means no. God does not regard peer pressure as a legitimate reason for giving in to temptation. Every person is responsible for his choices, even if the rest of humanity is in error.

> So then each of us shall give account of himself to God.

> —Romans 14:12

❧ Think over the last week. What temptations did you give in to? How did you justify those actions in your own mind?

❧ Now imagine that you are standing before God. Would you still give the same justifications for your actions? How might your view of temptation change in God's presence?

## ✐ "I Was Talked into It" ✐

People blame the influence of others for their behavior, saying such things as, "If it weren't for the people that I work with," or "My friend was so persuasive...." This is the same excuse that Adam tried to give. No matter how persuasive a person may be, in the end you are the one who decides what you will do. Until you are willing to face up to your personal responsibility regarding temptation and sin, you can change friends, jobs, and even families and still end up being molded and controlled by your environment. To put the blame for your habits on your circumstances or on other people is to allow someone else to control your destiny. You have handed the direction of your life to an entity that you cannot change and cannot control, and in the end it will fail.

> For we have spent enough of our past lifetime in doing the will of the Gentiles—when we walked in lewdness, lusts, drunkenness, revelries, drinking parties, and abominable idolatries. In regard to these, they think it strange that you do not run with them in the same flood of dissipation, speaking evil of you.

> —1 Peter 4:3-4

✐ When have you tried to break away from people who were a bad influence on you? What was their reaction?

✐ When have you chosen *not* to break away from such people? What was the result in your own life?

27

### ∾ "My Family is Cursed" ∾

We hear a great deal today about generational curses—about how the sins of the fathers are visited upon their children to the fourth generation (see Exodus 20:5). A number of people use this excuse for their weaknesses and sins, saying, "If you knew the kind of family that I grew up in, you would understand why I'm this way." But this is *not* an excuse for sin in the eyes of God. Parents and grandparents influence children, but in the end, children decide what they will *do*.

I was raised in a family situation that was far from ideal, and I know the weaknesses that can be woven into a personality from childhood. I understand the temptation to look to the past as an excuse to allow sin to go unchecked. But I also know the pain and frustration that such irresponsibility can cause to one's family and friends. I had to make a decision that I was going to leave the past behind and deal with things as they were. It was difficult, yet it was only after I took responsibility for my actions and asked God to help me change my behavior that I truly was able to make changes. I believe that will be true in your life, too, regardless of how you were raised or what kind of parents you had.

∾ In what ways do you believe that your parents influenced you to sin? What are you willing to do to reverse that trend in the future?

Fathers shall not be put to death for their children, nor shall children be put to death for their fathers; a person shall be put to death for his own sin.

—Deuteronomy 24:16

≈ According to this verse, how valid in God's eyes is our blaming sins on our family background?

### ∞ "This Sin is Acceptable in My Culture" ∞

There are those who believe that certain sins are acceptable for them because everybody in their immediate neighborhood or social group is engaging in it and has engaged in it for generations. This is only an extension of the peer-group and family-inheritance arguments. One's culture can be in error when it comes to the Word of God!

You shall therefore keep all My statutes and all My judgments, and perform them, that the land where I am bringing you to dwell may not vomit you out. And you shall not walk in the statutes of the nation which I am casting out before you; for they commit all these things, and therefore I abhor them.

—Leviticus 20:22-23

29

🐟 What sins are common in your culture today? What does God's Word say about these practices?

🐟 Which of those sins have you allowed into your own life? What does God say about things that violate His Word, even if they are legal and acceptable in your culture?

### ⤜⤛ "The Devil Made Me Do It" ⤜⤛

Some years ago, a popular comedian used the phrase, "The devil made me do it." This excuse, however, has been around since Eve. The truth of God's Word is that the devil has never forced any person to do *anything* contrary to his free will. The devil is a deceiver and the father of lies, but his only power over people is through manipulation and deceit. If he could actually make us do things, he wouldn't need to go to the trouble of deceiving us! If Satan could make us sin, the temptation process would be unnecessary. We will deal with the devil's role in the temptation process more fully later, but for now it is important to recognize that the devil cannot *make* us do anything.

But I fear, lest somehow, as the serpent deceived Eve by his craftiness, so your minds may be corrupted from the simplicity that is in Christ.

—2 Corinthians 11:3

🖎 Read Genesis 3:1-5. How did the serpent deceive Eve? How has he used the same lies to deceive you?

🖎 What does Paul mean by "the simplicity that is in Christ"? How does the "simplicity" of God's Word help you to resist temptation?

### ∞· "God Led Me into Sin" ·∞

Many people come to the conclusion that God has "led" them into sin because He allowed them to be born into a certain family or has given them a physical weakness of some type. The Scripture says clearly that God is not the cause of temptation. James 1:13 tells us:

> Let no one say when he is tempted, "I am tempted by God"; for God cannot be tempted by evil, nor does He Himself tempt anyone.

# Look in the Mirror

None of the excuses that we have looked at in this lesson holds water when it comes to justifying our sin before God. The plain and simple truth is that each person is responsible for his own actions and for his own sin. We have a free will with which we can choose to resist temptation or to give in to it. The only person to blame for sin is the person that you see in the mirror. As James 1:14 states, "Each one is tempted when he is drawn away by his own desires and enticed."

The decision that you must make today is whether you will continue to make these excuses and whether you will continue to attempt to "cover" for your own behavior. Some people believe that, if they can't fool God when it comes to their sins, they at least can fool others. That may be true, to an extent and for a limited time. But in the end, you *cannot* fool God and you *must not* fool yourself. Your own eternal destiny is at stake.

Keep your heart with all diligence, For out of it spring the issues of life. ... For as he thinks in his heart, so is he.

—Proverbs 4:23; 23:7a

When have you seen the connection between your thought life and your actions? Give examples.

Give examples of other ways that "the issues of life" have sprung out of your mental habits.

---

## Today and Tomorrow

TODAY: I ALONE AM RESPONSIBLE FOR THE CHOICES THAT I MAKE.

TOMORROW: I WILL STOP PUTTING THE BLAME ON OTHERS FOR MY OWN CHOICES, AND WILL ACCEPT MY RESPONSIBILITY BEFORE GOD.

# LESSON 4

# The Appeal

---------- ❧ **In This Lesson** ❧ ----------

*LEARNING:* WHERE DO TEMPTATIONS COME FROM IN THE FIRST PLACE?

*GROWING:* HOW CAN I GAIN STRENGTH IN RESISTING TEMPTATION?

---------- ∞ ----------

One of the most frightening passages of Scripture to me is Ephesians 6:11: "Put on the whole armor of God, that you may be able to stand against the wiles of the devil." This verse tells me two very important things: first, the devil has a plan that he has tested and perfected. His schemes worked against men such as David, Samson, Peter, Abraham, Jacob, and others. He is a skilled opponent. Second, the devil is out to destroy every believer. That includes you.

It is of the utmost importance, therefore, that we understand how the devil does his work so that we can resist him. We need to have as much knowledge as possible about his "appeal."

## The General Appeals that Satan Employs

The first thing that we must recognize is that Satan is in the business of deceit. Through his demonic cohorts, he is constantly working to convince us to buy into a lie. His lies are generally aimed at two areas of our humanity: our pride and our need for security.

### ∞ Our Pride ∞

From the beginning, Satan tempted mankind to establish an identity apart from God. Think about the implication of Satan's words to Eve in Genesis 3:4–6:

> Then the serpent said to the woman, "You will not surely die. For God knows that in the day you eat of it your eyes will be opened, and you will be like God, knowing good and evil." So when the woman saw that the tree was good for food, that it was pleasant to the eyes, and a tree desirable to make one wise, she took of its fruit and ate. She also gave to her husband with her, and he ate.

Satan was saying, in effect, "Eve, God has lied to you. You cannot always trust Him to do what is best for you. You need to begin looking out for yourself. It is time to make some decisions on your own and to be your own person. You can be like God. Why serve Him when you can be like Him? You don't need Him to take care of you. You can take care of yourself."

The appeal was to human pride, that we might abandon the place of significance offered to us by God and establish an identity of independence from God.

∞ When have you been tempted through an appeal to your pride and your desire for independence?

☙ Read through the specific lies that Satan told to Eve in the verses above. How does he still tell those lies today? Give specific examples.

## ❧ Our Need for Security ☙

Satan often tempts people by appealing to their need for security—the need to accomplish certain goals, possess certain things, be a part of a certain group, and so on. He tempts us to meet our needs through the ingenuity of our minds and the physical strength of our bodies, rather than relying upon God to meet those needs.

Satan tempts us with a lie: "If you only had..." or, "If you only did...." He couples the lie with a promise: "You would feel more fulfilled as a person, have greater self-confidence, and be more appealing to others." These two general appeals of Satan work because we are creatures of free will and are capable of making our own choices. In that, we do have a degree of independence from God and are responsible for our own decisions.

We also are responsible to a great degree for *using* the abilities and skills that the Lord has given to us, working to meet our needs as well as contributing to meeting needs in others. What is *not* true, however, is to think that we can ever be totally independent from God. We can never rely upon ourselves alone for our own provision. Our efforts to do so will not result in fulfillment but in feelings of frustration, disappointment, and dissatisfaction.

∾ When has Satan tempted you by promising greater "security" in a particular area of your life?

∾ **Partial Truth** ∾

Satan's generalized appeals to us are effective because he never tells the whole story, he never reveals the full outcome. He only gives the introduction to the first chapter of the story—the catchy, appealing "hook." He doesn't tell a person that if he takes a drink, he may end up an alcoholic, or that if she cheats on a test, she may wind up in prison one day for fraud. His appeal is always limited to a narrow, immediate opportunity to engage in sin.

Not telling the *whole* truth about a matter is a lie, and one of the foremost qualities of temptation is that it never deals with the *whole* of any particular situation.

### ∽ An Appeal to the Senses ∽

Satan's appeals to us are often sensory, based upon our sense perceptions and our physical needs and desires. These things are transitory and fluctuate in our lives, and Satan's temptations often come when we are weak or lacking in an area of physical need. The opportunities to yield to sin are also transitory and in fluctuation. But match up a person's weakness with an opportunity, and the setup is complete for temptation to be most effective.

> And the world is passing away, and the lust of it; but he who does the will of God abides forever.

> —1 John 2:17

∽ When have you given in to some physical temptation? How did you feel afterwards?

∽ How can it help to remember that all physical temptations and lusts are "passing away"?

# A Look at Your "Fleshly Desires"

We are not neutral targets for Satan. When Adam sinned in the Garden, the whole human race was polluted. Adam's decision to disobey God and to strike out on his own became interwoven into the fabric of humanity. Everybody is born with a tendency to sin. This is why you do not have to teach your children to sin—they are able to figure it out all by themselves!

This built-in mechanism lives in what the Bible calls the "flesh" (see Romans 7:18). When we become believers, the *power* of sin is broken, but the *presence* of sin remains. That means that believers do not have to give in to sinful desires, but those desires will still arise from time to time.

Satan's aim is to get us to satisfy God-given needs and desires in ways that are outside the boundaries of God. One of the truths that we must keep in mind as we combat temptation is that God has designed a way for our needs to be met. Our desires are, to a great extent, a reflection of the image of God. We have a desire for love, acceptance, respect, and success. And God has provided a way for us to experience the fulfillment of these desires.

We have a desire for food, for example. There is nothing wrong with eating—we must eat to maintain life and health. God provides us what we need through the bounty of the earth. Satan's temptation, however, is to convince people that they must overeat, eat the wrong things, or starve themselves out of fear of being overweight. His temptations play upon a very real God-given desire, but they are outside the boundaries that God has established for health.

Consider the example of sex. Sexual desire is from God, with the purpose of establishing a unique relationship between a man and a woman, and for the procreation of the human race. God says, "One man for one woman for life." Satan says, "Any man for any woman until you are ready for someone else." God says, "Sex is to be part of the marriage relationship." Satan says, "Sex *is* the relationship, and love is wherever you can find it for the moment." Satan is moving outside the boundaries that God has established for the fulfillment of our sexual needs.

The three foremost areas of the flesh in which the devil tempts us are:

1. *The lust of the flesh.* This area represents our appetites and desires. It includes the sexual desire but is not limited to it.

2. *The lust of the eyes.* This includes all those things that spark our desires and appetites, and especially those things that fuel our greed and our perceived need to acquire possessions.

3. *The pride of life.* This refers to anything that promotes or elevates a sense of independence from God—anything that causes us to think that we can have things our own way. It is especially strong in our need for power or control, as well as for recognition and praise from others.

> Do not love the world or the things in the world. If anyone loves the world, the love of the Father is not in him. For all that is in the world—the lust of the flesh, the lust of the eyes, and the pride of life—is not of the Father but is of the world.

> —1 John 2:15-16

✒ Give real-life examples of each of these sins:

Lust of the flesh:

Lust of the eyes:

Pride of life:

✒ When have you given in to each of these areas?

Satan's temptation of Eve involved these three target areas of the flesh. First, Satan appealed to Eve's pride (the pride of life). His promise was that her eyes would be "opened." Eve came to the conclusion that the tree was "desirable to make one wise." She was convinced that she would have greater insight, knowledge, and understanding. Satan also appealed to her desire for power and authority: "you will be like God." Eve knew that she and Adam had already been given a certain amount of authority—more authority seemed like a good thing, also.

Second, Satan appealed to Eve through what she saw (the lust of the eyes). We read that Eve saw that the tree was "pleasant to the eyes." Satan introduced intrigue and curiosity based upon what Eve saw. Her imagination was sparked. She had a desire to touch and possess and partake of what she saw.

41

Third, Satan appealed to Eve's basic need for food (lust of the flesh). We read that Eve saw that the "tree was good for food." She knew that she had to eat—why not eat of *this*?

Do you see the way that these three temptations are joined together? Rarely does Satan limit himself to one area of the flesh in tempting us. He points out something for us to *notice*—to see, to study, to contemplate. He fills our imagination with a visual image of something desirable. He then gives us a good *physical* reason to seek to act on that visual image, as well as a good *emotional* or *psychological* reason. He will convince us that we "need" to act on what we see.

Consider the example of a teen confronted with his first cigarette. He sees the use of cigarettes in movies and sees magazine and billboard advertisements. Then he sees a pack of cigarettes in the hands of a friend. Satan begins to whisper, "Look." Curiosity is aroused. Satan whispers, "This will make you popular. You'll have more importance in your peer group. And after all, isn't it time to make your own adult decisions?" The appeal is to the pride of life. Satan also whispers, "This will also make you calmer and more relaxed. And we all need something to help us cope with stress, right?" The appeal is to a basic lust of the flesh: the need for relaxation. The temptation is complete—all three appeals to the flesh have been made.

> Now the works of the flesh are evident, which are: adultery, fornication, uncleanness, lewdness, idolatry, sorcery, hatred, contentions, jealousies, outbursts of wrath, selfish ambitions, dissensions, heresies, envy, murders, drunkenness, revelries, and the like; of which I tell you beforehand, just as I also told you in time past, that those who practice such things will not inherit the kingdom of God.
>
> —Galatians 5:19-21

∽ Consider the list of sins in these verses. What element of the "flesh" is involved in each of them?

∽ What is the difference between "practicing" such sins and "falling into" them?

## The Element of Doubt

Added to the appeals that we have already discussed in this lesson, Satan also introduces an element of doubt. The account of Eve's temptation begins with Satan causing Eve to doubt. Doubt is often a major part of the temptation process, and at times it is the starting point for temptation to take hold.

So many people have come to me through the years with a story that includes lines such as, "If God doesn't want me to do this, then why do I feel the way I do?" or "If this isn't right, why hasn't God put a stop to it?" The element of doubt related to God's goodness, love, forgiveness, provision, or protection is always raised with the use of the word *if*.

The element of doubt generally results in our asking the question, "Why won't God let me fulfill my desire?" This is an extension of the "if" questions. "If God wants me to succeed, then why won't He let me fulfill my desire?" "If God wants me to have my sexual needs met, then why won't He let me fulfill my desire?" The problem with asking such "if" and "why" questions is that we add the phrase "in the way that I desire," so that our question really is, "Why won't God let me fulfill my desire in the way that I want to?"

The real questions that we should be asking are these:

    ◈ *"When* in God's perfect timing can I fulfill my desires?"

    ◈ *"How* would God prefer me to fulfill my desires?"

    ◈ *"What* means has God provided for me to deal with my desires in a way that is pleasing to Him?"

The truth of God is that He has a way for all of our desires to be met. He has a perfect timing, a perfect method, and a perfect "holding pattern" for us to maintain until His timing is right. The question is not whether God wants to meet our needs; the question that we must ask is, "What is God's best provision for meeting my need?"

Doubt takes root when we set our eyes on circumstances and we can't see how things are going to work out to our advantage. It is then that we often take matters into our own hands. The Lord asks us to trust Him, knowing that He will work things out for us—always for our good—and He asks us to keep His commandments as we wait patiently for His timing.

Blessed are the undefiled in the way, Who walk in the law of the LORD! Blessed are those who keep His testimonies, Who seek Him with the whole heart!

—Psalm 119:1-2

☙ What does it mean to seek God "with the whole heart"? When have you sought God with only half a heart?

☙ How can seeking God whole-heartedly strengthen you against temptation?

## The Easy, Quick Way

Satan's appeal to us nearly always promises that our needs will be met in the easiest, quickest, and least painful way. Satan offers us an "easy out." But most of the wonderful things in life take both time and sustained effort to develop and grow. That's true whether it's a marriage, a friendship, a business, a good habit, a reputation, a bond of loyalty, a good credit rating, health and fitness, and many other good things.

45

In our desire to avoid the effort and to shorten the time, we often fall prey to Satan's appeals. He offers a quick fix, an immediate high, instant gratification. He also offers us an immediate release from the anxiety that most people try to avoid. He presents ways for us to experience a "quick release" of built-up tension, frustration, or anger. At times, these solutions can seem in very good order—perhaps a buy-out of a company that you have built or some solution that seems to fit a portion of a problem.

The question that we must ask when "quick solutions" arise is, "What action on my part would bring God the greatest glory?" The *action* that we must take to determine the answer is to ask God to make His will known. When we have God's answer, we will also have peace about a decision. So many sins could be prevented if a person would only pause to ask, "What do *You* want me to do, Lord? Will this action on my part bring glory to You?"

God wants you to live without frustration and anxiety. But He has also made a way for that to happen. He does not promise to meet all of our needs immediately. What He promises is that He will mature us, conform us to the image of Christ Jesus, and provide His peace and strength to endure until all of our desires and needs are met.

The good news associated with Satan's appeals is that they are fairly obvious and predictable. Once we are fully aware of how Satan works, we are much better prepared to withstand him. To know one's enemy is truly the first step toward defeating him.

> Be anxious for nothing, but in everything by prayer and supplication, with thanksgiving, let your requests be made known to God; and the peace of God, which surpasses all understanding, will guard your hearts and minds through Christ Jesus.
>
> —Philippians 4:6-7

 What is the difference between "prayer" and "supplication"? Why does Paul add "with thanksgiving"?

 Why does God promise to "guard your hearts and minds"? Why doesn't He promise to grant our requests?

> For I delight in the law of God according to the inward man. But I see another law in my members, warring against the law of my mind, and bringing me into captivity to the law of sin which is in my members.
>
> —Romans 7:22-23

 What "law" is Paul referring to in our "members"? What does that law demand from us?

﹌ Read Romans 12:1-2. How can you rewrite that "law"?

> If you then, being evil, know how to give good gifts to your children, how much more will your Father who is in heaven give good things to those who ask Him! Therefore, whatever you want men to do to you, do also to them, for this is the Law and the Prophets.
>
> —Matthew 7:11-12

﹌ What "good gifts" would you like God to give you? List them below, with today's date, then start praying. When you receive an answer to each item, come back to this book and list it below.

﹌ Why does Jesus follow up this promise with a commandment on how we should treat other people? What is the connection between temptation and the ways that we treat others?

##  Today and Tomorrow:

*TODAY:* SATAN USES MANY TRICKS TO LURE ME INTO TEMPTATION, BUT JESUS HAS ALREADY DEFEATED HIM.

*TOMORROW:* I WILL BE ALERT THIS WEEK TO MY OWN LUSTS OF THE EYES AND FLESH, AND MY PRIDE OF LIFE.

## Notes and Prayer Requests:

# LESSON 5

# Our Defender

---
### ❧ **In This Lesson** ☙ ---

LEARNING: WHY DOES GOD ALLOW SATAN TO TEMPT ME IN THE FIRST PLACE?

GROWING: HOW CAN I HOPE TO DEFEAT THE DEVIL, WHEN HE IS SO MUCH STRONGER THAN I AM?

---

Satan is always on the offense against us. One of the most important things that you and I must do, therefore, is to have a solid defense against him. Ultimately, our defense is not in ourselves or in any other person or thing. Our defense rests with our Defender, our loving and omnipotent heavenly Father.

You may ask, "Well, if God is our Defender, why does He let the devil tempt us in the first place?" The reason comes back to free will. God has given man an opportunity to choose.

"But," you may counter, "I've already chosen Jesus as my Savior. Why must I continue to face temptation?" Because it is in withstanding temptation that we are made stronger in our faith and in our witness for the Lord. The Lord, therefore, *allows* Satan to tempt us for our ultimate benefit but, at the same time, He places limitations on Satan's power to tempt. Temptation becomes something of a "training tool" to cause us to grow up in Christ Jesus.

Will we ever reach the point in our spiritual maturity when we are not tempted? No. The apostle Paul warned us, "Therefore let him who thinks he stands take heed lest he fall" (1 Corinthians 10:12). We are each subject to temptation; no person is beyond it because there is always more room for each one of us to grow in Christ and to be conformed to an even greater degree to His character. Even so, God will not allow Satan to tempt us to the point where our defeat is assured or that God's purposes are thwarted.

## A Limitation on Satan's Temptation

In writing to the 1 Corinthians 10:12–13, the apostle Paul gives a promise concerning temptation. In his promise are two principles that give us insight into God's involvement in our defense against temptation.

Therefore let him who thinks he stands take heed lest he fall. No temptation has overtaken you except such as is common to man; but God is faithful, who will not allow you to be tempted beyond what you are able, but with the temptation will also make the way of escape, that you may be able to bear it.

### God limits the intensity of every temptation.

God knows you perfectly, inside and out, and He knows how much you can handle. He knows your breaking point. God knows your limitations, regardless of the nature of your temptation—finances, sex, anger, gossip, and so on. He promises to keep a watchful eye on the pressures that Satan brings against you. As you read through the following Scripture passages, note that Satan was granted permission to tempt and that a limit was set on the amount of pressure that Satan might exert.

And the Lord said, "Simon, Simon! Indeed, Satan has asked for you, that he may sift you as wheat. But I have prayed for you, that your faith should not fail; and when you have returned to Me, strengthen your brethren."

—Luke 22:31-32

Now there was a day when the sons of God came to present themselves before the LORD, and Satan also came among them. And the LORD said to Satan, "From where do you come?" So Satan answered the LORD and said, "From going to and fro on the earth, and from walking back and forth on it." Then the LORD said to Satan, "Have you considered My servant Job, that there is none like him on the earth, a blameless and upright man, one who fears God and shuns evil?" So Satan answered the LORD and said, "Does Job fear God for nothing? Have You not made a hedge around him, around his household, and around all that he has on every side? You have blessed the work of his hands, and his possessions have increased in the land. But now, stretch out Your hand and touch all that he has, and he will surely curse You to Your face!" And the LORD said to Satan, "Behold, all that he has is in your power; only do not lay a hand on his person." So Satan went out from the presence of the LORD.

—Job 1:6-12

Again there was a day when the sons of God came to present themselves before the LORD, and Satan came also among them to present himself before the LORD. And the LORD said to Satan, "From where do you come?" Satan answered the LORD and said, "From going to and fro on the earth, and from walking back and forth on it." Then the LORD said to Satan, "Have you considered My servant Job, that there is none like him on the earth, a blameless and upright man, one who fears God and shuns evil? And still he holds fast to his integrity, although you incited Me against him, to destroy him without cause." So Satan answered the LORD and said, "Skin for skin! Yes, all that a man has he will give for his life. But stretch out Your hand now, and touch his bone and his flesh, and he will surely curse You to Your face!" And the LORD said to Satan, "Behold, he is in your hand, but spare his life."

—Job 2:1-6

🐟 Why did God deliberately draw Satan's attention to Job? What purpose could this possibly serve?

🐟 Why did Jesus say to Peter, "when you return to Me"? What does this show of Jesus' love and forgiveness?

53

Satan, like all creatures, is subject to God's authority. We often don't think of him in that way. We tend to think of Satan and God on an equal plane, two equal forces pulling in opposite directions, yet Satan is a fallen angel, a creation of God. He is subject to God's authority.

In placing limits on our temptation, God assures us of three things:

1. *We will never be tempted more than we can bear*—not in our weakest moments, not even when we are tempted in our weakest area.

2. *God is involved in our struggle against temptation.* He isn't watching from a distance. He is functioning as a referee to the whole situation.

3. *God is faithful.* Even in our darkest hour of temptation, God does not turn His back on us. And no matter how we respond, God remains loyal in His love. In both our victories and defeats, He continues to keep the enemy in check.

☙ When has God caused a temptation to end "in the nick of time" in your life? When have you given in to temptation rather than looking for a way out?

### *God designs a way out of every temptation.*

No temptation is hopeless—we are always given a way to avoid falling into sin. Paul wrote that, when temptation comes, God "will also make the way of escape, that you may be able to bear it" (1 Corinthians 10:13).

Many people are able to anticipate when and where they will face temptation. They can say, "I know that, in the situation that I'm facing tomorrow, I am going to be tempted to this or that." In such cases, you should ask immediately for the Lord to reveal to you how you can escape that temptation! Even if you find yourself suddenly in an extremely tempting situation, you can trust that God has an escape plan for you. Ask Him to reveal it to you, and when He does, act on it. God will be faithful to provide a way of escape, but we must be faithful to look for it.

> No temptation has overtaken you except such as is common to man; but God is faithful, who will not allow you to be tempted beyond what you are able, but with the temptation will also make the way of escape, that you may be able to bear it.
>
> —1 Corinthians 10:13

How can it help you resist temptation if you remember that the temptation is "such as is common to man"?

↬ Note that God promises only to "make the way of escape" available. What is required of you?

# God Gives Us Power to Overcome

God limits our temptations and provides a way of escape, and He also provides us with the power to overcome temptation. Let me share three laws related to power:

1. *Power determines potential*. The potential to accomplish any particular task is determined by the power that we possess.

2. *Power must be harnessed and applied toward a specific goal before it serves any purpose*. Power in and of itself is useless. Its value lies in its application. The Colorado River, for example, has a great deal of potential power. But it is not until the river comes into contact with the turbines underneath Hoover Dam that the power of the river serves any useful function.

3. *Power, when harnessed and focused, can greatly extend the potential of the one who holds it*. Power becomes an extension of the one who controls and directs it. We might say that a lumberjack has enhanced potential when he has a chain saw in his hand—he has greater power to cut down trees and, thus, greater potential as a lumberjack.

Consider Paul's words in Ephesians 6:10–11:

> Finally, my brethren, be strong in the Lord and in the power
> of His might. Put on the whole armor of God, that you may be
> able to stand against the wiles of the devil.

Note that the power made available to the Ephesians was not human power—it was the power of the Lord. Paul encouraged the Ephesians that, as they received and used the power of the Lord, *they* would be made strong enough to stand against the devil. Their "potential" for winning against Satan was greatly enhanced. Paul makes this same point in Romans 8:12–14:

> Therefore, brethren, we are debtors—not to the flesh, to live
> according to the flesh. For if you live according to the flesh you
> will die; but if by the Spirit you put to death the deeds of the
> body, you will live. For as many as are led by the Spirit of God,
> these are sons of God.

Paul is saying that we have the power to say no to fleshly desires, but it is a power that is given to us by the Spirit. It is "by the Spirit" that we are to put to death the temptations that arise from our fleshly nature.

In Romans 6:14, Paul declares,

> For sin shall not have dominion over you, for you are not un-
> der law but under grace.

As believers in Christ Jesus, the Holy Spirit lives in us and we have power over sin. The conclusion that we can draw from these three passages of Scripture is a simple but profound one: *believers have a power greater than that of the devil, the flesh, or sin—it is the power of the Holy Spirit who indwells us when we receive Christ Jesus as our Savior.*

You are of God, little children, and have overcome them, because He who is in you is greater than he who is in the world.

—1 John 4:4

☙ If Satan was created by God (he was originally an angel
named Lucifer), then in what ways is the Holy Spirit greater than
the devil?

☙ If the Holy Spirit lives within you, then what powers are available to you in doing battle against temptation?

You may be saying, "Well, if God has given me all this power, why do I
keep giving in to the same temptations over and over? I pray and ask
God to help me, but I'm still so weak." Remember that power must be
*harnessed and applied* before it serves any purpose. *Having* the power
of God and *using* the power of God are two different things. James ad-
dresses this very issue in James 2:14, 20:

What does it profit, my brethren, if someone says he has faith
but does not have works? . . . Do you want to know, O foolish
man, that faith without works is dead?

58

James is not diminishing the role of faith—far from it. What he is saying, however, is that faith is useless unless it is applied. It accomplishes nothing unless it is *used* in a practical way for practical outcomes. God gives you access to His power, and He wants you to apply His power to overcome temptation. He is your full ally in the war against Satan. He makes available to you *all* of His resources. It is as if He has placed in your hands the very weapons that you need to win a victory over your enemy. He challenges you to pick up those weapons and use them!

✎ When have you been faced with a temptation that required you to do more than just believe in God's power, but to take a deliberate course of action yourself?

## Jesus Is Praying for You to Succeed

Jesus is praying that you will succeed in saying no to Satan's lies. We have the strong, active, and constant support of Jesus as our Defender. He is praying for us continually that we will be strengthened and kept safe from the enemy of our souls.

Jesus prayed for His disciples shortly before His arrest in the Garden of Gethsemane (John 17:14–17):

I have given them Your word; and the world has hated them because they are not of the world, just as I am not of the world. I do not pray that You should take them out of the world, but that You should keep them from the evil one. They are not of the world, just as I am not of the world. Sanctify them by Your truth.

We know that this prayer pertains to us as well, because Jesus also prayed that night, "I do not pray for these alone, but also for those who will believe in Me through their word" (John 17:20). That includes you and me! What a wonderful thing to know that Jesus is praying that we will not be overtaken by Satan. We are in this world for God's eternal purposes, and Jesus is praying that those purposes will be accomplished in us and through us until they are fulfilled.

Many people believe that God has somehow let them down or abandoned them when they are tempted. Nowhere does God promise to structure our lives so that we can avoid all temptation. He does, however, promise to help us withstand temptation, to provide a way out, and to keep us from being destroyed by the enemy.

Now this is the confidence that we have in Him, that if we ask anything according to His will, He hears us. And if we know that He hears us, whatever we ask, we know that we have the petitions that we have asked of Him.

—1 John 5:14-15

🔊 Give examples of things that you might ask God that are "according to His will". Give some examples of things that are *not* according to His will.

🔊 How can this freedom help you when faced with powerful temptation?

---

## 🔊 Today and Tomorrow 🔊

*TODAY:* GOD DOES ALLOW SATAN TO TEMPT ME, BUT HE ALSO BRINGS ME A WAY OF ESCAPE—EVERY TIME.

*TOMORROW:* I WILL SPEND TIME THIS WEEK MEDITATING ON GOD'S WORD, THAT I MIGHT BE STRONGER IN RESISTING TEMPTATION.

# LESSON 6

# Avoiding the Danger Zones

─────── ☙ **In This Lesson** ❧ ───────

*LEARNING:* WHERE CAN I FIND THE STRENGTH TO FIGHT BACK AGAINST
SATAN'S TEMPTATIONS?

*GROWING:* WHAT CAN I DO, IF SATAN'S POWER IS SO MUCH GREATER THAN
MINE?

─────── ⌘ ───────

Prevention is always the best cure. We know that to be true in many areas of our lives, and certainly it is a principle that extends to temptation. If we can *avoid* a tempting situation, we are wise to do so! I want to remind you of a central principle of the Bible: you as a believer have been made dead to the power of sin and alive in Christ.

## Dead to Sin

The apostle Paul was very candid in describing his battle with sin in Romans 7:14–17, 21:

> For we know that the law is spiritual, but I am carnal, sold under sin. For what I am doing, I do not understand. For what I will to do, that I do not practice; but what I hate, that I do. If, then, I do what I will not to do, I agree with the law that it is good. But now, it is no longer I who do it, but sin that dwells

in me ... I find then a law, that evil is present with me, the one who wills to do good.

All of us have experienced what Paul experienced. We know what we should do. At times, we even want to do it. Yet we cannot seem to find it within ourselves to do what is right. Unbelievers do not have the power to overcome sin in their lives consistently. For them, it is a futile struggle. For believers, however, it is a different story. Paul readily admitted to his *struggle*, but he also held out the great confidence made available to every believer in Romans 6:1–3:

> What shall we say then? Shall we continue in sin that grace may abound? Certainly not! How shall we who died to sin live any longer in it? Or do you not know that as many of us as were baptized into Christ Jesus were baptized into His death?

Then a few verses later (6:11), Paul writes,

> Likewise you also, reckon yourselves to be dead indeed to sin, but alive to God in Christ Jesus our Lord.

If the struggle persists, what does Paul mean when he says that believers in Christ Jesus are now "dead" to sin? It means that sin no longer has the power to *force* us to do or think anything. The power of sin still exists as an influence. The power of sin still has access to us, but it does not have any *authority* over us.

Some years ago, a friend gave our family a schnauzer puppy. My son, Andy, put a collar on the puppy's neck and proceeded to teach him how to sit down, lie down, and shake hands on command. He did this by saying, "Sit!" and, as he spoke, pushing the puppy's rear down while yanking his collar up. After some training, the puppy would respond to Andy on a verbal command only. The same thing happened with commands to roll over and lie down. Andy started the process of training by giving the verbal command, and then pushing or pulling on the puppy's collar to direct, reinforce, and exert authority for the command.

Satan has a collar around the neck of every unbeliever. When he commands, the unbeliever acts automatically. But when a person becomes a Christian, God removes the collar. Satan can still give the command, but the *power* of the command has been broken, the authority behind the command has been negated.

The problem is that many believers don't realize that the collar is off. They continue to respond the same way that they did when they were unbelievers. They don't realize that they can say no, and the Holy Spirit will enforce their "no" and give them the power to resist the devil.

What areas of temptation do you give in to almost automatically? When was the last time that you deliberately decided to resist that temptation?

Likewise you also, reckon yourselves to be dead indeed to sin, but alive to God in Christ Jesus our Lord.

—Romans 6:11

✍ Why does Paul tell us to "reckon ourselves" as being dead to sin? What does "reckoning," or mental attitude, have to do with temptation?

## Alive to Christ

Dying to sin is only half the story. The other half is that we are "alive to God in Christ Jesus our Lord." In accepting Jesus as our personal Savior, we had the collar of sin taken from us, *and* we received the indwelling presence of God to help us. Paul goes on to describe our new life further in Romans 6:3–7:

> Or do you not know that as many of us as were baptized into Christ Jesus were baptized into His death? Therefore we were buried with Him through baptism into death, that just as Christ was raised from the dead by the glory of the Father, even so we also should walk in newness of life. For if we have been united together in the likeness of His death, certainly we also shall be in the likeness of His resurrection, knowing this, that our old man was crucified with Him, that the body of sin might be done away with, that we should no longer be slaves of sin. For he who has died has been freed from sin.

To be baptized in Paul's time meant that a person was completely immersed into something. If a piece of cloth was "baptized" into dye, the cloth changed color. That's what happens when we accept Christ and are baptized in Him. Our nature changes completely, our identity changes, our outward expression changes. We are now indwelled by Christ, and the Holy Spirit lives in us to guide us daily into a victorious Christian life, and to prepare us for our eternal life with God in heaven.

We do not need to say yes to sin. We are free to say no to temptation. On the other hand, we must ask the Holy Spirit to act on our behalf and to help us both *avoid and withstand* evil every time it rises up. To avoid the danger zones of temptation, we must recognize first of all that we *can* avoid many temptations, and we *can* rely on the Holy Spirit to guide us away from tempting circumstances, people, or environments.

☙ Have you accepted Jesus as your Savior? If so, have you been baptized? If not, what is holding you back from becoming a Christian and being baptized now?

"Come now, and let us reason together," Says the LORD, "Though your sins are like scarlet, They shall be as white as snow; Though they are red like crimson, They shall be as wool."

—Isaiah 1:18

How does baptism symbolize the way that God completely changes a person's character when he is saved?

What effect does this change have upon your response to Satan's temptations?

## God Makes His Wisdom Available

In Ephesians 5:14–17, Paul identifies a number of sins that believers need to avoid:

"Awake, you who sleep,
Arise from the dead,
And Christ will give you light."
See then that you walk circumspectly, not as fools but as wise, redeeming the time, because the days are evil. Therefore do not be unwise, but understand what the will of the Lord is.

Our foremost prayer in avoiding temptation must be, "Lord, give me Your wisdom in how to avoid temptations." The Lord Himself taught us to pray this prayer: "Do not lead us into temptation" (Matthew 6:13). Jesus was saying, "Let us be led by You, Father, so that we won't even come close to temptation."

> If any of you lacks wisdom, let him ask of God, who gives to all liberally and without reproach, and it will be given to him. But let him ask in faith, with no doubting, for he who doubts is like a wave of the sea driven and tossed by the wind.
>
> —James 1:5-6

What sort of "reproach" do some people give if you keep asking for advice on the same topic? What do these verses suggest about the patience and gentleness of God?

Since God makes His wisdom so freely available, what does that suggest about your accountability before Him in resisting temptation?

We are to seek God's wisdom in every area of our lives, including:

1. *A careful appraisal of past results.* One of the questions that we should ask is, "What happened the last time?" It may be the last time you associated with a particular person, went to a certain place, or engaged in an activity. We are not wise if we refuse to learn from our past experiences.

2. *An understanding of your present weaknesses.* We are more susceptible to temptations when we are weakened in some way. For example, if we are very hungry, we can easily be tempted to eat the wrong foods or to eat too much. If we are very tired, we are more prone to doing something that will give us a quick boost. People who are committed to walking wisely stay in touch with their feelings, frustrations, and level of need. Every opportunity, invitation, and relationship should be evaluated according to one's present state of mind and feelings.

3. *A consideration of future plans, goals, and dreams.* Many temptations pale in light of one's future goals and dreams. Lying, cheating, stealing, gossiping, sexual sins—virtually all sins—affect what we will be able to do and the reputation that we will have in the future. The clearer our goals are in Christ Jesus, the more they can guide us away from sin.

4. *A sharp awareness of God's will.* Paul said to the Ephesians, "Understand what the will of God is." What he meant is this: "Don't go on willfully ignoring what God would have you do. Face up to it!" Paul is calling us to quit playing games, to quit excusing certain things in our lives that lead us into sin, and to quit rationalizing relationships that cause us to stumble.

Most people know enough about God's commandments to know right from wrong. They know what God wants them to do. What we need to do is to remind ourselves of what is right and then have the courage to *do* it. Ask God to give you both understanding and courage.

69

Have mercy on me, O Lord, for I am weak; O Lord, heal me, for my bones are troubled.

—Psalm 6:2

☙ When have you been faced with powerful temptation during a time of some physical weakness? How might you have avoided or reduced that temptation?

☙ Some weaknesses are beyond our own power. What does this Psalm say about those areas of weakness?

## Ask the Holy Spirit to Guide You Daily

The Holy Spirit functions much like the supreme "Tour Guide" of our lives—leading us to the paths that we should take and directing us to the things that we are to do. I encourage you to pray daily, "Holy Spirit, lead me where You want me to go, to say what You want me to say, and to do what You want me to do. Bring the right people and opportunities across my path."

The Holy Spirit works within us as the Spirit of truth. He convicts us of error, cautions us of impending danger, gives us the ability to discern spirits, reminds us of the words of Jesus Christ, and teaches us *how* to live a life that is pleasing to our heavenly Father. Invite the Holy Spirit to do His work in you! Ask Him to be the Spirit of truth, guiding and directing your every step.

> However, when He, the Spirit of truth, has come, He will guide you into all truth; for He will not speak on His own authority, but whatever He hears He will speak; and He will tell you things to come.
>
> —John 16:13

What is the role of the Holy Spirit? What specific things does He do, according to this verse?

In what ways can the Holy Spirit help you to deal with the specific temptations that you are presently facing? Be specific.

Let the word of Christ dwell in you richly in all wisdom, teaching and admonishing one another in psalms and hymns and spiritual songs, singing with grace in your hearts to the Lord.

—Colossians 3:16

☙ What does it mean to "let the word of Christ dwell in you richly"?

☙ How can the instructions in this verse be useful in resisting temptations?

───── ☙ **Today and Tomorrow:** ☙ ─────

*Today:* I need to remember that I am both dead to sin *and* alive to Christ.

*Tomorrow:* I will ask God to strengthen me and give me wisdom through His Holy Spirit every day this week.

# LESSON 7

# Dressed for Battle

---  ❧ **In This Lesson** ❧  ---

*LEARNING:* WHAT EXACTLY DOES "SPIRITUAL WARFARE" MEAN?

*GROWING:* IF I'M LIVING IN A WAR ZONE, HOW SHOULD I PROTECT MYSELF?

❈

Most Americans are quite fashion conscious. The Bible, however, speaks about a very different kind of wardrobe that we are to wear as believers. Paul describes this spiritual outfit in Ephesians 6:13–17:

> Therefore take up the whole armor of God, that you may be able to withstand in the evil day, and having done all, to stand. Stand therefore, having girded your waist with truth, having put on the breastplate of righteousness, and having shod your feet with the preparation of the gospel of peace; above all, taking the shield of faith with which you will be able to quench all the fiery darts of the wicked one. And take the helmet of salvation, and the sword of the Spirit, which is the word of God.

This is a popular passage among preachers, and most Christians are familiar with it. I find very few, however, who take seriously Paul's application of these verses. Paul did not say, "Understand the full armor of God," nor did he say, "Research each piece of Roman armor alluded to in these verses." Paul said about this armor, "Put it on!"

# Dressed for War

One of the reasons that people fail to overcome temptation is that they are unprepared for Satan's attack. They aren't expecting the devil to come after them in a warlike fashion, with a fierce intent to kill and destroy.

We've all heard the phrase "dressed to kill." Paul's variation on that phrase would be that Christians are to be "dressed for war." Most of us never think about dressing for war. And most of us never think about the fact that we *need* to put on the armor of God because we are under attack continually. Paul was very clear in stating, "Put on the whole armor of God, that you may be able to stand against the wiles of the devil" (Ephesians 6:11). Our enemy is known. His tactics are known. And he is continually launching an assault against us!

In preparing ourselves for war, we must not be like a soldier who has his mind elsewhere in the heat of battle. We must be alert to the task at hand: defeating the devil. We must remain focused on this as one of our prime purposes in life—to confront and defeat Satan on this earth.

✒ Consider each piece of armor which Paul describes in the passage above. What does each piece do? How is it used?

Girdle (belt or sword belt):

Breastplate:

Boots:

Shield:

Helmet:

Sword:

## ∽ The Pieces of Our Armor ∽

Before we get into the actual application of the pieces of armor that Paul described, we need to know what they are:

1. *The abdomen covered by a girdle of truth.* Roman soldiers wore a girdle-like belt around their waists. It was actually more like an apron than a belt. It was made of thick leather, and it covered the entire abdominal region. It also supported the soldier's sword.

Truth is the foundation for everything that we do as believers. The truth is what gives us hope when we face temptation. The truth is what allows us to rely fully on God's power as we face the enemy. It supports what we believe and is the basis for what we believe. The girdle protects that region of the body that produces life and is most closely connected to the movement of God's Spirit within a person; so also the truth is what must govern our lives. It is on the Spirit of truth, the Holy Spirit, that we rely.

∽ When has your "girdle of truth" been missing when you faced temptation? What element of God's truth did you fail to follow?

2. *The chest area covered by a breastplate of righteousness.* Breastplates were usually made of leather, although some of them were studded or covered with metal. The breastplate protected the chest region and all the vital organs. In the ancient world, people believed that the emotions resided somewhere in a person's chest. The breastplate is associated with righteousness because what is right often conflicts with what we feel. The breastplate of righteousness guards us from making decisions based on what we feel rather than what we know to be right. So often temptation begins in our emotions. We must keep our emotions in check so that they are used as God intended for them to be used.

When was your breastplate of righteousness missing when you faced temptation? How did your emotions lead you into disobeying God's Word?

3. *Feet shod with the gospel of peace.* The foot covering of the Roman soldier was a thick leather sandal wrapped around both the foot and the ankle with leather thongs. The shoe is associated with peace because we are to have peace as our motivation wherever we go, and in our wake, the "footprint" that we leave should be one of peace.

When have you yielded to temptation because you did not have peace as your motive?

**4.** *One hand holding a shield of faith.* The shields used by the Roman soldiers were very large. In fact, the word translated as "shield" comes from the word that meant "door." Roman shields were made with an iron frame that had leather stretched over it. Some were also covered with metal pieces. A soldier could kneel down behind such a shield and be completely protected in the front. On occasion, the Romans would soak their shields in water so that any flaming arrows that struck them would be extinguished.

Faith is associated with the shield because it is our defense against fear, insecurity, and any form of criticism or abuse that might be launched against us from an enemy. Faith is our assurance that, no matter what a person may say about us or do to us, we are children of God, beloved by God, and redeemed by the blood of Jesus Christ. We do not need to take into our spirit the hurtful remarks of others; we can say in the face of them, "I believe in God and in His Son, Jesus Christ, and all else is only temporary and fleeting."

✎ When have you yielded to temptation because your shield of faith was not up—not relying upon the Lord to quench the fiery remarks or deeds of another person?

5. *The head covered with the helmet of salvation.* A helmet was a soldier's most costly and ornate piece of armor. It was designed to protect the entire head.

The mind is where most of our battles are won or lost. It is there that the decisions about behavior are made, and we decide whether we will obey or disobey. We are saved from temptation when we choose with our minds to be obedient. Our salvation is what gives us the potential to say "yes" to God and "no" to sin. In so doing, we are saved, in a temporal sense, from the act and consequence of sin.

When have you yielded to temptation because you willfully chose to sin?

6. *One hand grasping the sword of the Spirit.* This is the only offensive weapon that is listed in the armor of God. The Roman sword was shorter and broader than a fencing sword. The Word of God is viewed as a sword because of its power to overcome the onslaught of the enemy. We will deal with this more in the next lesson, but for now we should note that the Word of God is what sends Satan and his hosts running for cover.

When have you felt at a loss as to what to say to a tempter?

No Roman soldier would have dreamed of going into battle without these six pieces of equipment secured and ready for action. To do so would have meant certain death. Paul knew that believers dared not enter into spiritual warfare without being fully prepared as well!

～ Putting on the Armor ～

How do we actually put on this spiritual armor? We do it the same way that we engage in virtually all spiritual practices: we use our faith and our words.

First, you must *believe* that God desires to protect you from the enemy who comes to stalk and defeat you through temptation. You must believe that Jesus is your full provision—the One who is your Salvation, the One who gives you peace, the One who imparts righteousness, the One who gives you the Spirit of truth. You must believe that God has given you His Word to use. Putting on the armor of God is putting on a new awareness of Christ Jesus. One person described it this way: "It's like putting on a new coat of belief, just like putting on a new coat of paint." It is covering your mind and heart again with a full awareness of who Jesus is and what He has done for you.

Second, you must *state* what it is that you believe. This pattern of saying what you believe is seen throughout the New Testament. Paul wrote in Romans 10:9–10, "If you confess with your mouth the Lord Jesus and believe in your heart that God has raised Him from the dead, you will be saved. For with the heart one believes unto righteousness, and with the mouth confession is made unto salvation."

What we believe establishes our minds. What we *say* establishes our behavior—it becomes our "stance" in the world. The connection between what we believe and what we say is very important. It dictates what we will eventually do!

Every morning I say the following prayer. This may look like a long prayer, but you will probably find that it can be said in about three minutes. I encourage you to read this prayer aloud, alone or as a group.

Good morning, Lord. Thank You for assuring me of victory today if I will follow Your battle plan. By faith I claim victory over .... [I list some of the things that I will be facing that day.]

To prepare myself for the battle ahead, by faith I put on the belt of truth—the truth about You, Lord, that You are the sovereign God who knows everything about me, both my strengths and weaknesses. Lord, You know my breaking point and have promised not to allow me to be tempted beyond what I am able to bear. The truth about me, Lord, is that I am a new creature in Christ and have been set free from the power of sin. I am indwelt with the Holy Spirit who will guide me and warn me when danger is near. I am Your child, and nothing can separate me from Your love. The truth is that You have a purpose for me this day—someone to encourage, someone to share with, someone to love.

Next, Lord, I want to put on the breastplate of righteousness. By faith, I strap on this breastplate to guard my heart and emotions. I will not allow my heart to attach itself to anything that is impure. I will not allow my emotions to rule in my decisions. I will set them on what is right and good and just. I will live today by what is true, not by what I feel.

Lord, this morning I put on the sandals of the gospel of peace. I am available to You, Lord. Send me where You will. Guide me to those who need encouragement or physical help of some kind. Use me to solve conflicts wherever they may arise. Make me a calming presence in every circumstance. I will not be hurried or rushed, for my schedule is in Your hands. I will not leave a trail of tension and apprehension. I will leave tracks of peace and stability everywhere I go.

I now take up the shield of faith, Lord. My faith is in You and You alone. Apart from You, I can do nothing. With You, I can do all things. No temptation can penetrate Your protecting hand. I will not be afraid, for You are going with me throughout this day. When I am tempted, I will claim my victory out loud ahead of time, for You have promised victory to those who walk in obedience to Your Word. So by faith I claim victory even now because I know there are fiery darts headed my way even as I pray. You already know what they are and have already provided the way of escape.

Lord, by faith I am putting on the helmet of salvation. You know how Satan bombards my mind day and night with evil thoughts, doubt, and fear. I put on this helmet that will protect my mind. I may feel the impact of his attacks, but nothing can penetrate this helmet. I choose to stop every impure and negative thought at the door of my mind. I elect to take every thought captive; I will dwell on nothing but what is good and right and pleasing to You.

Lord, I take up the sword of the Spirit, which is Your Word. Thank You for the precious gift of Your Word. It is strong and powerful and able to defeat even the strongest of Satan's onslaughts. Your Word says that I am not under obligation to the flesh to obey its lusts. Your Word says that I am free from the power of sin. Your Word says that He that is in me is greater than he that is in the world. So by faith I take up the strong and powerful sword of the Spirit, which is able to defend me in time of attack, comfort me in time of sorrow, teach me in time of meditation, and prevail against the power of the enemy on behalf of others who need the truth.

So, Lord, I go now rejoicing that You have chosen me to represent You to this lost and dying world. May others see Jesus in me, and may Satan and his hosts shudder as Your power is made manifest in me. In Jesus' name I pray, Amen.

You may choose to pray the whole armor of God onto your life in different words, but this is a sample of how such a statement can be made in prayer. Something happens when we *state* our beliefs. We grow stronger inside. We have a greater resolve. We have an increased motivation.

Be sober, be vigilant; because your adversary the devil walks about like a roaring lion, seeking whom he may devour.

—1 Peter 5:8

What does it mean to "be sober"? Why is soberness important in fighting the devil?

How would the pieces of Roman armor, described above, help in fighting a lion? How does the armor of God help in defeating the "roaring lion" of temptation?

## ∞ Putting First Things First ∞

I can't imagine going out to preach without having on my socks and shirt. I make sure that I am properly dressed *before* I step into a pulpit. The time to put on spiritual armor is *before* you encounter temptation, not after temptation comes. Furthermore, Paul did not *suggest* that we put on the whole armor of God. He *commanded* us to do so. He knew that even one missing piece of armor puts a person at a disadvantage that could cost him an important spiritual victory.

No matter how you choose to put on the spiritual armor of God, you will do so by your faith and by your verbal confession of what you believe. Make this a top priority, one of the first things that you do every day. It worked for Paul, and it has worked in my life. I am confident that it will make a difference in your life as you seek to win victories over temptation.

> You therefore must endure hardship as a good soldier of Jesus Christ. No one engaged in warfare entangles himself with the affairs of this life, that he may please him who enlisted him as a soldier.
>
> —2 Timothy 2:3-4

∞ What sorts of hardship would a foot soldier need to endure? How does this hardship compare with what you face each day?

෨ What "affairs of this life" are you entangled with at present? How are these entanglements interfering with your spiritual warfare?

---
## ෨ Today and Tomorrow ෨

*Today:* I cannot hope to defeat Satan if I'm not fully dressed in the armor of God.

*Tomorrow:* I will begin to pray daily, putting on my spiritual armor before anything else.

---

## ෨ Notes and Prayer Requests: ෨

# LESSON 8

# Wielding the Sword

──────── ❧ **In This Lesson** ☙ ────────

LEARNING: WHY IS THE BIBLE COMPARED TO A SWORD?

GROWING: HOW DO I *USE* THE BIBLE LIKE A SWORD?

✿

My favorite hobby is photography. An ideal vacation to me is loading up all my camera equipment and taking off for a couple of weeks on a photographic safari. In my endeavor to increase my skills as a photographer, I have learned some important lessons. One of them is that there are no problems unique to me as a photographer. Whatever predicament I find myself in, some other photographer has already wrestled with the same dilemma. I have also learned that the best way to save myself hours of headache is to ask a pro how he deals with a problem.

We are wise to apply this same approach to temptation, asking ourselves, "Who has struggled with the same problem and dealt with it successfully?" The answer is given in Hebrews 4:15:

> For we do not have a High Priest who cannot sympathize with our weaknesses, but was in all points tempted as we are, yet without sin.

If we are looking for an expert who has had experience with temptation and has overcome it successfully, we need to look no farther than Jesus! He is the master in this area. Matthew 4:1–2 tells us, "Then Jesus was led up by the Spirit into the wilderness to be tempted by the devil. And when He had fasted forty days and forty nights, afterward He was hungry."

Jesus had withdrawn into the wilderness, led by the Spirit. For one month and 10 days, Jesus had gone without food in the course of His intense prayer. At the end of 40 days and 40 nights, He was hungry. Most of us would say that we were "starving" at that point! Jesus was probably weak from not having eaten. He was no doubt drained emotionally from His prolonged time in prayer. All of His physical and emotional energy would have been at a low ebb. We have mentioned in previous lessons that temptations often come when we are feeling "low" physically or emotionally. If there was ever a time to tempt the Lord Jesus, this was it—and Satan knew it.

## The Ultimate Temptation

Now when the tempter came to Him, he said, "If You are the Son of God, command that these stones become bread."

But He answered and said, "It is written, 'Man shall not live by bread alone, but by every word that proceeds from the mouth of God.'"

Then the devil took Him up into the holy city, set Him on the pinnacle of the temple, and said to Him, "If You are the Son of God, throw Yourself down. For it is written: 'He shall give His angels charge over you,' and 'In their hands they shall bear you up, Lest you dash your foot against a stone.'"

Jesus said to him, "It is written again, 'You shall not tempt the Lord your God.'"

Again, the devil took Him up on an exceedingly high mountain, and showed Him all the kingdoms of the world and their glory. And he said to Him, "All these things I will give You if You will fall down and worship me."

Then Jesus said to him, "Away with you, Satan! For it is written, 'You shall worship the Lord your God, and Him only you shall serve.'"

Then the devil left Him, and behold, angels came and ministered to Him.

—Matthew 4:3–11

🖎 Notice the three temptations that the Lord faced. What different areas of life was Satan trying to appeal to?

🖎 How did Jesus respond to each area of temptation?

## ∞ Jesus' Ultimate Response ∞

*Jesus did not make one original comment during His entire interaction with the tempter.* This is amazing to me. The Son of God—the One who knows all things and has the power to do all things, the One whose words we study, memorize, and meditate on—chose to respond to temptation using the truth of His Father's Word. The three passages that Jesus quoted were from God's Law in the Old Testament (Deuteronomy 8:3; 6:16; and 6:14).

*Jesus' use of the Word of God was effective.* The plain truth of God's Word was enough, directed at the deception behind each of Satan's enticements. No creative arguments were required. Jesus simply quoted the Word of God to Satan, and that was enough to make him withdraw.

These two truths are very liberating to me. They mean that I don't have to outsmart Satan. I don't have to discuss things with him. I don't even have to muster up enough raw willpower to fight Satan. I simply have to know the Word of God and then to speak it to him.

> Now the serpent ... said to the woman, "Has God indeed said, 'You shall not eat of every tree of the garden'?" And the woman said to the serpent, "We may eat the fruit of the trees of the garden; but of the fruit of the tree which is in the midst of the garden, God has said, 'You shall not eat it, nor shall you touch it, lest you die.'" Then the serpent said to the woman, "You will not surely die. For God knows that in the day you eat of it your eyes will be opened, and you will be like God, knowing good and evil." So when the woman saw that the tree was good for food, that it was pleasant to the eyes, and a tree desirable to make one wise, she took of its fruit and ate....
>
> —Genesis 3:1-6

 How does Satan's temptation of Eve compare with his temptation of Christ?

 How does Eve's response to the devil compare with Jesus' response?

## The Power of the Word of God

There are four reasons why a well-chosen passage of Scripture is effective against temptation.

1. *God's Word exposes the sinfulness of what you are being tempted to do.* One of Satan's subtle snares is to convince you that what you are being tempted to do is not really a sin. Satan has a smooth way of rationalizing sin away. When we turn to the Word of God for an answer to Satan, we are confronted with the truth. There was nothing inherently wrong with Jesus desiring bread. After all, He had been without food for 40 days. What was wrong was for Jesus to put His personal needs above obedience to the Father. The verse that He quoted was saying, "My ultimate responsibility is not simply to satisfy My physical needs, but to obey My Father in heaven." The truth of God's Word exposed the sinfulness of what Satan was requesting.

The same thing will happen when we turn to the Word of God for an answer to Satan's temptations. You will see clearly what is at stake. God's Word takes you right to the heart of the matter and allows you to see things for what they really are.

When have you been tempted to sin because an argument seemed rational? What Scripture passage would have refuted that argument?

Your word I have hidden in my heart, That I might not sin against You.

—Psalms 119:11

How does a person "hide" God's Word in his heart?

**2. God's Word gives God's objective viewpoint on the situation.** The Scriptures provide us a divine perspective. We will say to a friend, "Give me your objective opinion." Well, if we want a truly *good* objective opinion, we need to look to the Word of God. That's where we get God's perspective.

Too often we can get caught up in strong, emotional feelings that make us vulnerable to temptation. The truth of Scripture pulls us away from our emotions to a position of objectivity.

> Through Your precepts I get understanding; Therefore I hate every false way. Your word is a lamp to my feet And a light to my path.
>
> —Psalm 119:104-105

What is the difference between "a lamp to my feet" and "a light to my path"? Why does the Psalmist emphasize both the path and the feet that are walking on it?

How is God's Word like the "lamp" and "light" analogies?

3. *God's Word causes us to focus our minds.* It is impossible *not* to think about something. Stop reading for a moment, and try your best not to think about pink elephants. You won't be able to do it. I have planted that idea, and you will at some point have at least a fleeting image of a pink elephant in your mind! We are thinking all the time, and we cannot avoid thinking. What we must do, therefore, is to focus our attention on those things that are good to think about.

One of the surest ways to avoid temptation is to turn your thoughts toward God's Word the first moment that a temptation enters your mind. Eve's biggest mistake was talking things over with Satan. She should have repeated back to him verbatim what God had commanded her to do and then just walked away.

> Finally, brethren, whatever things are true, whatever things are noble, whatever things are just, whatever things are pure, whatever things are lovely, whatever things are of good report, if there is any virtue and if there is anything praiseworthy— meditate on these things.
>
> —Philippians 4:8

 Define the following attributes of good thinking, and give examples of each.

True:

Noble:

Just:

Pure:

Lovely:

Good report:

Virtue:

Praiseworthy:

4. *When we voice God's Word, we are activating our faith.* When we turn to God's Word and quote it to Satan, we are actually pulling the "on" switch for our faith. As we discussed in the previous lesson, there is a dynamic connection between what we believe and what we say, and a direct connection between what we say and what we do. Our faith is ignited when we *speak* God's Word to the tempter. Nothing moves God like the active faith of His people.

> My tongue shall speak of Your word, For all Your commandments are righteousness.
>
> —Psalm 119:172

In the coming week, try speaking God's Word out loud each time you face temptation. Then list below what the temptation was, what Scripture you quoted, and what resulted.

## Building Up an Arsenal

To be able to speak the Word of God to the tempter, one must first *know* the Word of God. The moment of temptation is not the time to go running for a concordance to find an appropriate Scripture passage. We must have the Word of God living in us. We must memorize God's Word so that we have key verses ready when temptations arise. These verses are like arrows in a quiver, like the gleam on the Sword of the Spirit (see Ephesians 6:17).

I know Christians who spend hours figuring out crossword puzzles, but they don't have time to study the Word of God. I know Christians who know dozens of phone numbers off the top of their head, but they contend that it is too hard to memorize the Scriptures. Ask God to help you become more disciplined in your reading and memorizing of the Bible, and then begin to take action.

To combat the onslaughts of the enemy effectively, you need an arsenal of verses on the tip of your tongue—verses that are so familiar that they come to your mind without any conscious effort.

> My son, if you receive my words, And treasure my commands within you, So that you incline your ear to wisdom, And apply your heart to understanding; Yes, if you cry out for discernment, And lift up your voice for understanding, If you seek her as silver, And search for her as for hidden treasures; Then you will understand the fear of the LORD, And find the knowledge of God.

> —Proverbs 2:1-5

Notice the verbs in these verses. Define each and give practical examples of how to do it.

Receive my words:

Treasure my commands:

Incline your ear:

Apply your heart:

Cry out for discernment:

Lift up your voice for understanding:

Seek [wisdom] as silver:

Search for [wisdom] as for hidden treasures:

Find verses that apply to you, then memorize them. Find verses that:

*Deal specifically with the area in which you are most often tempted.* If you recognize that you are most prone to lying, cheating, giving in to anger, and so forth, find a verse that speaks God's truth about this situation.

*Address the issue of lust.* Men especially should have several verses on the tips of their tongues that have to do with lust or immorality. We all are bombarded at every turn with the promise of pleasure through illicit sex.

*Speak the truth of God about gossip.* It is very easy for us to participate in pointless chatter about other people.

*Remind us of our Christian duty to obey the laws of our government and to respect those in authority over us.*

Here is a small sample of passages to get you started.

*Gossip:* James 1:26

*Lust:* Psalm 119:9; Proverbs 6:24-33; Galatians 6:7-8; Colossians 3:2-3

*Fear:* Psalm 56:3; John 14:1

*Disobey parents:* Ephesians 6:1-3

*Demand your own way:* 1 Corinthians 6:19-20

*Hiding sin:* 2 Corinthians 5:10

*Worry:* John 16:33

Once you have memorized a verse, keep it fresh in your memory by reviewing it frequently. Meditate on what the verse means *to you*. Think about specific ways that the verse applies to your life. I once heard about a young boy who had memorized a great deal of the Bible who was also caught stealing money from the church offering plate. When the pastor confronted the boy, he began by quoting him a verse on stealing. The boy quickly pointed out that the pastor had slightly misquoted the verse, but he failed to see any connection between the verse and his behavior. Memorizing Scripture isn't enough. You must see how it relates to your personal life!

## The Renewal of Your Mind

Paul speaks of filling our minds with Scripture, calling it the "renewal of the mind." He writes in Romans 12:2:

> Do not be conformed to this world, but be transformed by the renewing of your mind, that you may prove what is that good and acceptable and perfect will of God.

Each of us wants to know what God considers to be *good*. Each of us wants to engage in what God considers to be *acceptable* behavior. Every Christian I know wants to do the will of God—the *perfect* will of God. The way to discover what God desires for us, and to walk in that way, is to study God's Word with regularity, focus, memorization, and meditation, until the Scriptures become the way that we think.

We have considered the connection between what we believe, say, and do. That link flows from belief to speech to action, but it also flows from action to speech to belief. What we do reinforces the meaning of what we say, and what we say reinforces what we believe. A positive cycle is created that results in a genuine transformation of our minds.

97

Set your mind on things above, not on things on the earth.

—Colossians 3:2

How does a person "set his mind" on something? Give examples of things that you have set your mind to accomplish in the past.

How can memorizing Scripture help you to set your mind on the things of God?

---
### ✍ Today and Tomorrow ✍

*TODAY:* I CAN ONLY FIGHT THE SPIRITUAL BATTLE IF I'M WELL-ARMED BEFOREHAND.

*TOMORROW:* I WILL SPEND TIME THIS WEEK FINDING AND MEMORIZING VERSES THAT ADDRESS MY PERSONAL AREAS OF TEMPTATION.

---

# LESSON 9

# No Lone Rangers

---
### ◆ In This Lesson ◆

LEARNING: IF GOD IS FIGHTING ON MY BEHALF, WHY SHOULD I SHARE MY SECRETS WITH OTHER PEOPLE?

GROWING: HOW DO I FIND SOMEONE THAT I CAN TRUST WITH MY PERSONAL STRUGGLES?

---

God never intended that any of us should be spiritual lone rangers. He wants us to develop a personal relationship with Him through His Son, Jesus Christ, and He also desires that we be in close association with other believers who will build us up, admonish us at times, and befriend us always.

The final stage in developing a strong self-defense against temptation is *accountability* to others. Accountability is a willingness to provide an explanation of one's activities. Each of us is accountable to someone in some way. On the job, we are accountable to our employers. In our communities, we are accountable to the government in the way that we keep its laws. Children are accountable to their parents, and when they are in school, they are accountable to their teachers. Morally and ethically, we are accountable first to God and second to the entire body of Christ.

Many people balk at this, saying, "My moral conduct is nobody's business. That's between the Lord and me." But is it really? We have mistakenly come to believe that, since God promises to help us when we are tempted, we don't need to mention our temptations to anyone else. Temptation is a private thing, after all.

But as private as temptation may be, *sin is rarely private.* Sin eventually reaches out beyond the confines of an individual life and touches others around it. Even those things that you consider to be "only in your mind" will eventually influence the way that you think, speak, and act to others.

To whom are you accountable for various aspects of your life? Consider all areas, including family, work, community, etc.

How do you feel about being accountable to others in the body of Christ?

# An Effective Deterrent

When we are in close affiliation with other believers, we have an effective deterrent against temptation and sin for several reasons:

1. *We have an outlet for talking about the feelings and frustrations that may lead us to sin.* Talking about our inner feelings often keeps a person from acting on those feelings. This outlet may be temporary, but sometimes a temporary "bandage" is enough to help us examine the root issues of the problem.

Many extramarital affairs have little to do with sex. Pressures at home and work can build to the point where one or both spouses are so concerned about their own needs that they fail to communicate and to spend time *talking and listening* to each other.

~ When have you avoided sin by talking to someone about your feelings or problems?

2. *We have someone who will pray for us.* When you are part of a group of believers who are accountable to one another, you have a built-in support system of those who will help you in your battles.

☙ When have you stood strong against temptation by praying with someone or asking someone to pray for you? Are you aware of others who may have interceded on your behalf to keep you from sin?

3. *We quickly discover that we are not alone in our temptation.* The apostle Paul made this point in 1 Corinthians 10:13: "No temptation has overtaken you except such as is common to man." Knowing that you are not alone in your temptation relieves some of the pressure.

☙ When have you discovered that you were not alone in a problem or temptation?

4. *We find that we have a source of wise counsel.* Often the experience of others can provide us with great insight about how to approach a particular temptation. Pooling the wisdom and creativity of a group of believers always gives birth to new ideas and solutions. You have probably discovered this as you have worked within your current small group on this topic of temptation. Those who are "accountability partners" have the advantage of objectivity and fresh insight. They may also bring to your attention key verses of Scripture that you had not thought to memorize previously.

At times, the wise counsel of a group may come in the form of practical information that a person had not known. A woman in a church that I once pastored was married only a short time when she discovered that her husband was involved in a homosexual relationship. She told me that, after she and her husband divorced, several of her friends came to her and said that they knew he was involved in homosexuality before their wedding.

"I asked them why they didn't tell me. They said, 'We didn't think it was any of our business.'" Her friends were dead wrong. They violated a scriptural principle of sharing the truth with someone in order to help that person. We *are* our brother's keepers. This does not mean that we have a right to be nosy, but it does mean that, when we have information that would be helpful to a person, we should be willing to share that information freely.

The warnings and admonitions that we give to others must be given in a spirit of love and help, never in a desire for manipulation; but they should be given openly and freely as opportunities arise in the course of your "accountability partnership" with one another.

꙳ How have others helped you live a godly life—either by admonishing you against sin or encouraging you to act righteously?

Brethren, if a man is overtaken in any trespass, you who are spiritual restore such a one in a spirit of gentleness, considering yourself lest you also be tempted.

—Galatians 6:1

Let the word of Christ dwell in you richly in all wisdom, teaching and admonishing one another in psalms and hymns and spiritual songs, singing with grace in your hearts to the Lord.

—Colossians 3:16

꙳ What principles do these verses give for holding others accountable?

## Choosing an Accountability Partner

The Bible does not give us any rules that govern when and how often we should meet with other believers for accountability purposes. My daughter, Becky, met with an accountability partner once a month, and they stayed in touch by phone between meetings. My son, Andy, met with his accountability partner once a week over breakfast. One pastor on our staff met with an accountability group once a week. Some of the teenagers in our church meet during lunch at school. Accountability partners don't have to hold formal meetings, but they do need to discuss their lives with one another on a periodic basis and be willing to discuss openly all issues and subjects.

Your best accountability partner will probably be a person with whom you have something in common. It should be someone of your sex. It should be someone whom you respect spiritually. This does not mean that your partner needs to be a Bible scholar or pastor, but your accountability partner should be someone who is seeking to gain God's perspective on life.

One thing that you do *not* want to have is a relationship with someone who criticizes you every time you get together. Neither do you want someone who will never confront you. A balance needs to be struck between encouragement and exhortation, with far more encouragement than exhortation. I suggest that you and your partner make a decision never to give opinions unless asked for them—and then be free in asking for opinions!

No person in the body of Christ should be a "Lone Ranger." We each need someone who will know us and whom we cannot deceive. We each need someone who will accept us as we are and yet challenge us to become more like Christ. We each need a friend on whom we can depend fully. Ask God to bring such a person into your life. If you already have such a friend, be open to ways in which you might deepen your friendship and hold each other to even greater degrees of accountability.

> Open rebuke is better Than love carefully concealed. Faithful are the wounds of a friend, But the kisses of an enemy are deceitful.
>
> —Proverbs 27:5-6

> He who rebukes a man will find more favor afterward Than he who flatters with the tongue.
>
> —Proverbs 28:23

☙ What sort of "wounds" might come from a faithful friend? What sort of wounds would *not* come from a faithful friend?

Why do we tend to have more respect for someone who re-bukes us than for someone who flatters us? What is required of the "rebuker" for this to be true? What is required of us when we are rebuked?

---

### Today and Tomorrow

*TODAY:* NOBODY CAN HOPE TO FIGHT AGAINST TEMPTATION WITHOUT HELP FROM OTHER CHRISTIANS.

*TOMORROW:* I WILL ASK THE LORD TO BRING ME TOGETHER WITH AN-OTHER BELIEVER WHO CAN BE MY ACCOUNTABILITY PARTNER.

---

# LESSON 10

# Misunderstandings About Temptation

---

### ☙ In This Lesson ☞

*LEARNING:* IS IT REALLY A SIN TO BE TEMPTED?

*GROWING:* CAN I EVER OUTGROW TEMPTATION?

---

In my years of pastoral work, I have repeatedly encountered six theories regarding temptation, none of which can be supported biblically but all of which seem to enjoy widespread belief. These misunderstandings cause many well-meaning believers to live under a burden that God never intended them to bear. Consequently, they become discouraged and unmotivated. Each is a distortion of the truth, and therefore I believe that Satan is the source of these misunderstandings.

## Six Misunderstandings

In Paul's writings to the Corinthians, he points out that ignorance of Satan's schemes allows Satan to take advantage of believers (see 2 Corinthians 2:11). I believe that a misunderstanding in the area of temptation does just that: it sets up a person to be deceived and to become discouraged.

We'll take a look at each of these misunderstandings in this final lesson. There will be very few Scriptures cited in this lesson for the primary reason that the misunderstandings which we are going to cover do *not* have a basis in Scripture, and therefore they have no scriptural support. We need to be aware of these misunderstandings, however, so that we are not led astray from the truths which we have covered in previous lessons.

## Misunderstanding 1: "Temptation is a sin."

The first misunderstanding is that it is a sin to be tempted. People who believe this often feel guilty for sins that they haven't committed solely on the basis that they have been tempted. The truth is that we are not responsible for what flashes through our minds. Our responsibility is to control the things that *dominate* our thoughts. Paul clarifies this difference in 2 Corinthians 10:4–5:

> For the weapons of our warfare are not carnal but mighty in God for pulling down strongholds, casting down arguments and every high thing that exalts itself against the knowledge of God, bringing every thought into captivity to the obedience of Christ.

If God expected us to be able to control what came into our minds in the form of perceptions, fleeting ideas, or sensory information, He would not have instructed Paul to write to the believers to "take every thought captive." He would have had Paul write, "Shut the door completely to all thoughts that might be negative." Our responsibility lies in sifting thoughts and in determining which thoughts will be allowed to take root in our minds and hearts. We are to dwell on the good and drive out the bad.

Our environment determines to a great extent what comes into our minds. Even the most cautious people will at some point be exposed to things that will summon ungodly thoughts and feelings. We cannot control what other people wear, say, or do at all times. We cannot control what we are invited to participate in (although we obviously can control what we choose to participate in). We cannot control what we accidentally overhear. All of these things are thrust upon us without our consent.

Some of the things that we hear pack an emotional punch, and when our feelings get involved, we often become confused. We need to stop and recognize that an emotional response is a natural, God-given gift to us as human beings. It is our responsibility to weigh our emotional response and the external stimuli, and then to determine what sort of action we will take. No sin has taken place until we say or do something in response to stimuli.

Jesus Himself was tempted, and Jesus never sinned. He was completely righteous, even though He was tempted, and therefore we can safely conclude that it is *not* a sin to be tempted.

➤ See 2 Corinthians 10:4–5, above. What are some examples of "carnal weapons"? What weapons do we fight with?

☙ How, in practical terms, does a person "bring every thought into captivity"? What spiritual weapons are useful in this?

## Misunderstanding 2: "Temptation ends when we become spiritually mature."

I am always amazed at how people respond when I share that I may be struggling in my personal life. They make an assumption that spiritually mature people are not harassed by temptation. That is certainly not the case.

All of us will face temptation for the rest of our lives. There is no escaping it. We have the idea that our ultimate goal as Christians is to reach a point where we are never tempted. Ironically, the very opposite is true. The more godly we become, the more of a threat we become to Satan, and the harder he works to bring us down! A mark of spiritual maturity is that a person does not *sin* when faced with temptation, not that a person *has* no temptations.

One of the things that we need to realize is that our struggle against temptation can produce something *good* in our lives. Spiritual maturity is not defined by whether or not we are tempted; what matters is what we do in the face of the temptation and what we experience as a result of overcoming the temptation.

> My brethren, count it all joy when you fall into various trials, knowing that the testing of your faith produces patience. But let patience have its perfect work, that you may be perfect and complete, lacking nothing.

> —James 1:2–4

How would it be helpful if you were to "count it all joy" when you are faced with temptation? How might that strengthen you to resist?

What does patience have to do with resisting temptation? How does James' formula actually help us to grow stronger at resisting temptation?

## Misunderstanding 3: "Temptation should eventually cease."

A closely related misunderstanding is that, once we have dealt with a particular sin or habit, all temptation in that area will subside. Again, this misunderstanding is rooted in the concept that Christians can come to the point where they experience no temptations whatsoever.

Often, Christians struggle with a particular sin for a long time, even years or decades. They may go through a period when they believe that they have gained a definitive victory over a particular habit, addiction, or problem, and then—WHAM! The old feelings and thoughts come back around.

If this happens to you, I encourage you to check your own Christian disciplines. Have you been reading your Bible and praying daily? Have you remained in close fellowship with other Christians? Are you involved in ministry to people or in service to the church? Often, old temptations come back during times when a person has been lax in his good spiritual habits. At other times, temptations arise when a person allows himself to become overly tired, extremely stressed, or "burned out." If this is the case, then shore up the area of your defense system that has been breached.

You must also recognize that the Lord has never promised to deliver you from being tempted. He has only promised to help you resist temptation and to overcome it. If you are tempted time and time again with the same temptation, don't automatically assume that you have a deep, underlying problem. Neither should you assume that you are any more "sinful" than anybody else. Nowhere in Scripture is a person's spirituality judged on the basis of frequency of temptation. The truth is that we are all weaker in some areas than in others. Satan will always seek to capitalize on our weaknesses.

✍ When have you felt guilty because an old habit of sin suddenly cropped up as a temptation after years of dormancy? In what ways are you able to let go of that guilt today?

✍ How are your daily Christian disciplines right now? Are you reading the Bible and praying daily? Meeting with Christians regularly?

## Misunderstanding 4: "We simply 'fall' into sin."

I often hear people say, "You know, I was going along just fine, and then suddenly I *fell* into sin." Such terminology makes it appear that Christians are victims, innocent bystanders, who get swept into sin against their will. That is not the case. No matter how much pressure we are under, no matter how enticing the temptation, no matter how repeated the temptation, we each have sufficient will to say no and to stand by that no *if we will choose to rely upon the Holy Spirit to help us.*

No Christian falls innocently into sin. The Holy Spirit will convict us every time that we are about to sin or that we have taken the first step toward sinning. We *choose* to sin. In every incident of temptation there is a point at which we cast a deciding ballot either to sin or not to sin. No person has ever been forced, kicking and screaming against his will, to give in to temptation. We must face up to the fact that we are personally responsible for our sin and that there is no justification for our sin other than the fact that we *choose to sin.*

What is the difference between "falling prey to temptation" and "falling into sin"? What elements of personal choice are involved in each of those areas?

⤙ When have you experienced sudden, unexpected temptation? Did you resist or give in? What motivated your choice?

### Misunderstanding 5: "God is disappointed in us when we are tempted."

I have met people who harbored very strong guilt because they were tempted. They felt that God was disappointed in them and that He was shaking His head in disgust over their temptations. My question to them is this: "Do you think that God was disappointed in His own Son when He was tempted?" Certainly not.

When we feel disappointed in ourselves, we often assume that God is disappointed as well. Such, however, is not always the case. God does not expect you to live a temptation-free life and, therefore, God cannot be disappointed when you *do* experience temptations. God knows about every temptation that has come your way and that will come your way. Nothing takes Him by surprise. Furthermore, temptation is one of God's tools to develop character and faith in believers, as we noted earlier in James 1:2–4. When we are tempted, we have an opportunity to overcome temptation and emerge with stronger faith and character. James 1:12 tells us:

Blessed is the man who endures temptation; for when he has been approved, he will receive the crown of life which the Lord has promised to those who love Him.

We are *rewarded* when we resist temptation and persevere through it. The fact that we are tempted does not grieve God; He is grieved only when we give in to temptation.

~ What does James mean when he says "when he has been approved"? What does God's approval have to do with temptation?

~ According to this verse, what might we do that would *not* gain God's approval? How does this reflect on the idea that God is disappointed in you when you face temptation?

## Misunderstanding 6: "It's possible to get away from all temptation."

Many people believe that, if they can just stay away from all sinful environments, they will be able to live a temptation-free life. I have met people who frequently change jobs, churches, or even move from city to city in an effort to escape temptation. They nearly always end up in a situation very similar to the one which they just left—because they changed their circumstances, but they did not renew their own minds.

The territory for temptation is not external. It is internal. Temptation is not waged on a particular geographical or environmental battlefield. It is waged on the battlefield of the mind. The only way to overcome temptation and to resist the devil is to stand firm in your heart and mind in the midst of temptation.

God has not taken those who believe in Jesus Christ out of this world; rather, He calls us to be in this world and to take a stand against evil and for righteousness at every turn. If you spend all of your time trying to avoid temptation, you will become too isolated from society to have any impact on it. There is a time to run and a time to stand!

> I beseech you therefore, brethren, by the mercies of God, that you present your bodies a living sacrifice, holy, acceptable to God, which is your reasonable service. And do not be conformed to this world, but be transformed by the renewing of your mind, that you may prove what is that good and acceptable and perfect will of God.
>
> —Romans 12:1-2

☙ What does it mean to "present your bodies a living sacrifice"? What does this have to do with temptation?

☙ What effect would "renewing your mind" have on certain temptations? Give specific examples of temptations that you face, and how a renewal of thinking might influence them.

# And If We Fail?

What are we to do if we fail to overcome temptation and actually engage in sin? First, we must confess our sin to God immediately and ask for His forgiveness. Do not say to yourself, "Well, now that I've sinned, I may as well keep sinning." Put an immediate stop to your sin. Go to the Lord and admit, "Lord, I have sinned against You. Please forgive me."

Then we must receive the Lord's forgiveness by faith and forgive ourselves. We must stop looking at our past and begin to look to our future.

A third step is also important. We must ask the Holy Spirit to help us not to yield to this temptation in the future. We must ask for His help daily as we build a strong defense against temptation. We also must:

✎ Learn the lessons that God wants to teach us in the aftermath of our failure.

✎ Make amends with any person whom we may have hurt in our sin.

✎ Be open to sharing with others the dangers of temptation and the consequences of sin, always with a humble heart, a thankfulness for God's forgiveness, and wisdom in knowing what to share and what not to share.

Consider what David prayed in Psalm 51:10–13:

> Create in me a clean heart, O God,
> And renew a steadfast spirit within me.
> Do not cast me away from Your presence,
> And do not take Your Holy Spirit from me.
> Restore to me the joy of Your salvation,
> And uphold me by Your generous Spirit.
> Then I will teach transgressors Your ways,
> And sinners shall be converted to You.

Allow God to use your failures to do a transforming work in your life and to draw you into closer intimacy with Him. Allow your failures to create in you an even more intense desire to withstand the devil and to overcome future temptations. God loves you always. And He always stands ready to forgive and to heal you when you come to Him with a humble heart.

> "These things I have spoken to you, that in Me you may have peace. In the world you will have tribulation; but be of good cheer, I have overcome the world."
>
> —John 16:33

➤ If Jesus has already overcome the world, what effect does this have on the temptations that you face?

How can a strong sense of Jesus' peace help to strengthen you in facing temptation? Encourage you when you fail?

And now, little children, abide in Him, that when He appears, we may have confidence and not be ashamed before Him at His coming. If you know that He is righteous, you know that everyone who practices righteousness is born of Him.

—1 John 2:28-29

What does it mean to "abide" in Christ? In practical terms, how is this done?

🕭 What might make you ashamed when standing before Jesus? How can this perspective help you in resisting evil?

---

### 🕭 Today and Tomorrow ॐ

*TODAY:* GOD IS NOT DISAPPOINTED WHEN I AM TEMPTED—ONLY WHEN I *YIELD* TO TEMPTATION.

*TOMORROW:* I WILL WORK ON RENEWING MY MIND SO THAT I CAN GAIN GOD'S PERSPECTIVE ON SIN AND TEMPTATION.

## Notes and Prayer Requests: